R50,00

D0118958

Wilderness DAWNING

To Beverly

for without air under its wings,
a bird cannot fly.

Wilderness
DAWNING

Peter Pickford

C·STRUIK

Contents

C. Struik Publishers (Pty) Ltd
Struik House, Oswald Pirow Street
Cape Town 8001

Reg nr. 80/0284/07

Copyright © Peter Pickford

Designed by Abdul Amien, Cape Town
Typeset and lithographic reproduction by Hirt & Carter (Pty) Ltd, Cape Town.
Printed and Bound by Tien Wah Press (Pty) Ltd, Singapore

All rights reserved. No part of this publication may be reproduced, stored in a retrieval system or transmitted in any form or by any means, electronic, mechanical, photocopying, recording or otherwise, without the written permission of the copyright holder.

ISBN 0 86977 493 x

First published 1987

The quotation on page 13 is taken from Richard Shelton's *The Tattooed Desert* (1971) University of Pittsburgh Press, Pittsburgh, Pennsylvania, USA; that on page 40 from Rudyard Kipling's *The White Man's Burden;* that on page 66 from *The Lowveld, its History and its People* by Colonel J. Stevenson-Hamilton published by Cassel Ltd, UK; that on page 92 from General J.C. Smuts' Foreword to *The Lowveld, its History and its People;* that on page 114 from Credo Mutwa's *Indaba My Children,* Blue Crane Books, Johannesburg; that on page 139 from Ansel Adams' *The Portfolios of Ansel Adams,* Little, Brown and Company, Boston, Massachusetts, USA; and that on page 160 is also from *The Tattooed Desert* by Richard Shelton. Where relevant, permission has been sought from the copyright holders concerned.

Foreword

Many years ago my telephone rang one morning and I was told by my secretary that a lady wished to talk to me about her son. I was under great pressure at the time trying to find money for the 3rd World Wilderness Congress and the Wilderness Leadership School. It was a never-ending grind that seemed to eat up my energy.

I was about to say, "Tell the lady to phone another day, I really don't have time to talk to anyone today." Then something inside me said, "A boy is looking for direction." I had long learned to trust my intuition, so I talked to the lady. It was Peter Pickford's mother who told me about her son and how he wanted to work in "the bush". It was a request that many mothers had made over the years and I had always tried to help, but there was a limit to the number one could assist. But my intuition was pressing and I agreed to find a place for Peter Pickford, but to test the lady's bona fides and my own intuition I said he would have to pay in order to work on a game ranch. Mrs Pickford was silent for a moment, as though taken aback that one had to pay in order to work. Then she agreed and Peter went to the Hluhluwe district to work with an old friend of mine, Maurice Mackenzie.

I saw Peter once or twice after that and then there was a long silence until one day I met him at the Sabi-Sabi Game Reserve. He was happy and enjoying his work and he was grateful for the training he had received on the Hluhluwe game ranch.

More years passed, then I was telephoned by Peter Pickford and asked if I would open a photographic exhibition of his in Durban. Again there were other pressing matters but I agreed because intuition said "do it."

When I saw Peter's photographs I knew that the wilderness had touched his soul. Photography of wild places, people, animals and birds was his way of responding. In some strange way I felt it was a repayment of the trust I had placed in him years ago. One could always take from the wilderness but if there was no effort to repay the debt to nature of being allowed to see some of her secrets, the *amadhlozi* (spirits) as the Zulus called the ancient ancestors, would never be satisfied. Peter Pickford had responded and had produced photographic art in tribute.

Recently, Peter phoned again, and this time he asked me to do a foreword to his book. Twice I refused, my workload being very heavy, but on the third request intuition took over and said "do it."

I apologise for the lengthy preamble but it is important that the reader of this book should know that Peter Pickford is not simply an ordinary photographer. It has been a long haul for him in a tough school.

In *Wilderness Dawning* Peter Pickford has proved that not only is he an outstanding photographer but he can write too. His prose is gripping and again it is apparent that during the days and nights spent in the Zululand and Eastern Transvaal lowveld amongst the game and in drought, heat and cold and thunderstorms, the spirit of this ancient continent of ours reached out and fired him to express his love for it.

The reader may well ask where does the fiction begin and the non-fiction end? I believe it is unimportant because what Peter Pickford is showing and telling us is part of the story of some of the people who lived and travelled in the acacia savannah lands east of the Drakensberg mountains, the Bushmen, the Nguni, the Portuguese and the others who followed. In tiny pockets like Sabi Sand, Timbavati, Klaserie, Umbabat, Sabi-Sabi, Londolozi, Mala-Mala, Kruger National Park, remnants of the ancient story remain. Very few who pass through in a vehicle or fly over in an aeroplane can read or hear the story of the old people. Peter has, and in doing so he has repaid his obligation, whether it be in fact or in fiction.

Wilderness Dawning is an expression of Peter Pickford himself and comes from the depth of his inner being. I trust that other books will come, infused always by the wilderness spirit.

Dr Ian Player D.M.S.

A shy and secretive recluse of the dense canopies of riverine forest, the purplecrested loerie rarely reveals its striking plumage. But when it does venture out, its flight is punctuated with sporadic bursts of scarlet splendour.

Photography

Many cities are alike, many a farmland reminiscent of another. There is no parallel for an African wilderness. Its character evades satisfactory description. In some it courses through the veins with the fever of obsession and for those prepared to attempt to reach out and touch it, the experience is awesome and humbling.

The pages of this book reflect my response to that intangible. They are not an attempt to document geography and natural history but are intended more as a subjective exploration of the aura of an African wilderness.

I came before reality not only to portray the blatant and exciting but to delve deeper into the subtleties and nuances, on a quest for the soul of my subject.

Representations without doctrine, each photograph is presented as a means unto its own end, while remaining an inexorable part of the whole. Each is a moment in the expanse of time, a scene from a broader canvas, a facet of the whole that is an arena without equal.

That the book is incomplete in this regard, I acknowledge without reserve for the palette is boundless and my approach was unshamedly subjective.

Acknowledgements

It is with deep appreciation that I extend my sincerest gratitude to the following: Patrick and Jenny Shorten and their magnificent staff for their immeasurable kindness and assistance and their remarkable tolerance; Mitch Reardon who said "Yea! You've got a book!" and more; John and Sheila Nicholls who so kindly gave us the use of their camp as a base from which to work; David Wright who got me to dig in the dirt and gave me a new understanding of the wilderness; Tony Hardwick who was still able to smile as my vehicle limped in for yet another repair; Nick Zambatis, Phil de Kok and Piet Muller of the Hoheisen Research Institute for their remarkable attitude and unflagging support; Nick and Tim Hancock for the use of their camp in the Timbavati; Erwin Liebnitz, Mike Brereton and Trevor Thompson, the wardens of the various reserves, for their co-operation and guidance; Mario and Megan Cesare for their hospitality and enthusiasm; Mr Harry Kirkman for bringing the old days to life; the committees of the reserves and to the many members, too numerous to mention, whose kindness and support made the production of this book possible; Roy and Val Wise for the use of their cottage at Mbona, which provided the necessary seclusion for me to write; Terry Carew for his willing help; the members of the Stevenson-Hamilton Library for their enlightened assistance during the research of this book, Hilton Cohen who worked during a holiday to fly me over the reserves; Johan Froneman who so readily gave me the use of his aeroplane; June Vincent for deciphering my scrawl and typing the manuscript; Abdul Amien whose quiet, understated talent transformed a jumble of photographs, desires and convictions into a book; Peter Borchert and Wim Reinders of Struik for all that they gave in the production of this book, but above all for an enthusiasm that matched my own; those many, many people from whose encouragement I was able to draw so much strength; and last, but by no means least, to my parents who first showed me the wilderness, and to the late Colonel Stevenson-Hamilton to whom so much is owed.

Note
For the sake of the story it has been necessary to omit passages of history which I hope the reader will forgive. Apart from Manukosi, Shaka and João Albassini, all characters and incidents are imaginary and any resemblance to persons living or dead is entirely coincidental.

Introduction

I fled. Not to, but from. I was being borne along in the mindless current of society's expectations where success loomed over my head like a demigod.

What I found enthralled and enchanted me. Africa benign, ancient and brooding, mother of none but mistress of many, with the subtlest of wiles, claimed yet another victim.

All too fast, civilization is digging its fingers into the recesses of the world and leaving conformity in its wake. Africa, a continent of intrigue and fascination, is losing its individuality as modernization blankets its face. The trepidation of pioneers who sought the mysteries of this quondam land, that taunted and tempted them, is gone as the tarmac of highways covers the footpaths of elephants. Already too much of Africa is in museums. Even more is remembered only in ancient songs that none sing and only the wrinkled hum in their hearts, for it is an embarrassment to remember what man has squandered so that he might prosper. Too often history has proved the soil to be more precious than the gem it yielded.

In the evening of this century – a century that has seen man's most rapid progress – he still has not come to terms with his greed. Perhaps only when he too is dying, will he realize that extinction is for ever.

When the dust of our passing has settled, there will be those who walk behind and see the tin cans and the plastic, for that is what we made for them. I hope they will also see a forest, and know, that this, too, we left for them.

Conservation, not only of natural realms but also of cultures, is a gesture of selflessness on which the charisma of Africa rests. In contemplation of his place in time, man must realize how far he has to go, and that it is not his right to usurp the majesty of a continent.

Peter Pickford
Cape Town, June 1987

Previous page: A study in concentration. Embraced by the branches of a dead marula and a warm winter sun, a cheetah searches for prey.

A plain of lush, gently swaying grass becomes charged with tension as a cheetah begins its first stalk of the day.

I must have been almost crazy to start out alone like that on my bicycle pedalling into the Tropics carrying a medicine for which no one had found the disease and hoping I would make it in time.

Richard Shelton

The DAWNING

Night falls suddenly in the lowveld. It brings with it an air of intrigue and discomfort as man's primary sense, his sight, fails him. It is the prickling sense of unease felt as one swims in unknown waters for the first time.

As the sun sinks away over the western horizon and darkness comes, warthogs arrive at their burrows. Turning, they reverse down into their homes and protection for the night. A greenspotted dove sings its final lament to the day. For a while all is still. A herd of impala bunches closer together. Then, as the short twilight fades, the eerie call of a jackal lifts off the plains and floats out to greet the darkness. A world wrapped in secrecy, the African night unfolds.

A hyaena arches its neck towards the ground. The unmistakable whoop, to so many the herald of Africa's wild realms, vibrates down its throat. The cat-like predators yawn and stretch sinewy muscles that ripple below their skin. The night is theirs as their pupils dilate, absorbing all available light and giving them an advantage over their prey. A scuffle is accompanied by a soft rattle as a porcupine forages in the undergrowth. Other unusual creatures appear to feed beneath the stars. A pangolin advances slowly on its back legs, scratching the ground here and there with its long foreclaws, its hard scales clinking like ancient armour. An aardvark scurries for cover, short powerful legs carrying its stocky body at great speed.

For many it is a time of fear as death walks with the moon. A mouse fidgets uncomfortably, its long whiskers twitching nervously. A metre or so away a genet stands motionless on its back legs, ears twisting to and fro as it strains for a sound. Suddenly it pounces, jumping high into the air. It lands with paws on the mouse, its jaws snap closed.

As the night wears on, its creatures take time to rest. The lesser bushbaby and its larger cousin, the thick-tailed bushbaby, cease foraging in their lofty tree-top domain and curl up in the fork of a tree until a few hours before dawn. A leopard straddles a branch, panting from the effort of dragging a fully grown impala ram high into a tree. Hyaenas sniff at the base, salivating as a meal dangles beyond their reach.

Silence. The fire crackled and spat. An ember drew a red and gold arc and died before it hit the sand. A murmur escaped from the leaves above. My chair scraped slightly as I pulled it closer to the warmth.

The old man continued to stare fixedly into the fire. The flames that danced sporadically above the coals cast the lined skin into etched relief and showed a face that once must have been quite ugly.

Time had softened the harsh features of youth, and years spent outdoors had given a not unpleasant leathery appearance to the tanned, slightly blotchy skin. A halo of fine silvery hair framed the face, plastered to the scalp in a thin band above the ears by the battered hat that was now uncharacteristically sitting on his knee.

With the unhurried deliberation of someone who has lived a life free from the pressure of urgency, he began patting his pockets. He stopped at his left coat pocket, fumbled briefly in the folds of the fabric and withdrew a pipe. After sucking on it, he hawked softly and spat into the coals. The fire sizzled and hissed in retaliation.

"She would never allow me to do that," he said. The hint of a smile touched his mouth and accentuated the wrinkles around it. It was not a smile at new-found freedom, for his wife had been dead for many years, but a glimpse of an attachment that could still affect him after all his time alone.

He swivelled slightly in his chair, straightening his leg, and dug in his trouser pocket for his tobacco pouch. With the movement his hat toppled from his knee and on to the sand. He retrieved it with his left hand, dusted it against his trousers and placed it on his head.

He filled the pipe, tapping it down with his index finger, the tip of which had been crushed in a long-ago accident.

"I've been thinking about what you youngsters were discussing the other night," he said. (He referred to anyone more than ten years his junior as 'youngster'.) He took his time finding a twig with which to light his pipe, allowing the full meaning to sink in.

On that night, we had all thought him asleep in his chair and had been amazed at his ability to slumber on through a discussion that had sometimes become quite heated. He had apparently been awake, but had chosen not to show it, content just to listen.

Lifting the flaming twig to his pipe, he drew gently. His eyes twinkled with amusement from beneath his bushy eyebrows.

"It is necessary," he said, once he had the pipe going, "to put your discussion into perspective and to do that we must go back, way back, in time."

He puffed contemplatively on his pipe with his eyes closed for a full minute. I had learnt long ago not to interrupt him at this stage for he stood fast to his belief that one should know what one wanted to say before saying it and he was now rallying his thoughts. He viewed interruptions with ill-concealed contempt.

Grunting to himself, he opened his eyes. He moved his hands outwards in an expansive gesture and began.

Stretching out from the foot of the escarpment, the country rolled in gentle undulations to the horizon. Here and there a hill or rocky outcrop punctuated the scene. They had names then but these have been long forgotten and replaced with others. The sun, also known by a different name, had climbed into a cloudless, hazy sky.

A vulture circled slowly in a gentle thermal of the early morning. Far below him the golden brown veld was interspersed with patches of green. The focus of his attention, however, was on three yellow-brown bodies that moved, now upright, now crouching, through the grass. The bird feared the animals that walked upright but also knew that if they were followed for long enough, there was bound to be food for the picking.

On the ground, Xi touched his brothers on their shoulders and pointed to the bird poised high above them. Smiles creased their faces. It was a good omen to hunt under the blessing of the 'bird that sees all'.

The tracks of the kudu bull were very fresh and the San hunters crouched lower and lower in the sea of grass, slowing to a walk the easy pace that they had kept up since dawn.

Xi's hand goes out in a signal and he freezes. Across a small clearing the kudu browses, unaware of the imminent danger. His horns rattle on the branches as he reaches deep into a thicket for some choice leaves. Suddenly he starts as if stung and gallops off with his tail raised in alarm, showing the white underside.

His gallop slows to a trot and then a walk. He stops in an open area near a dry pan, and tests the wind, staring intently in one direction after another for several minutes. Apparently satisfied, he nudges with his nose at the source of irritation but this causes more pain. The skin on his flanks shakes in a shiver and he stamps his leg but the arrowhead holds fast. The poison on its tip has seeped into his blood now and he staggers slightly as he stares again at the bush. He tries to walk around the pan, but stumbles on the rough ground. His head starts to drop and he splays his legs to maintain his balance. He is stung again, and this time tries to swing around to face his tormentors, but the poison has taken effect and he crashes to the ground.

The need for concealment gone, the three San burst from the grass with a chatter of staccato, self-congratulatory clicks. Soon a small fire is burning and some choice pieces are roasting while the kudu is butchered into three portions to be carried back to the caves. Care is taken to leave a portion for the 'bird that sees all' and the threesome set off homeward.

The tragedy and the triumph of this late winter morning have been repeated for centuries. Man, no less an animal, has played his part. ☐

I realized now that I was to experience one of the old man's rare monologues. Given more to listening than talking, he nonetheless possessed the rare gift of story telling, and tonight he had a tale to tell. His eyes were fixed unseeingly on some object above the fire as he continued his story.

The band of three arrived back in their valley after the warmth had left the sun, and was greeted by excited naked children. The kudu was admired, but it was overshadowed by the news brought by the women who had been digging for bulbs. They had seen a group of many, many people in a valley two days away from their caves.

Late that night, with bellies distended from a feast of kudu and bulbs, the San sat outside their caves in the liquid, colourless light of the moon and discussed this mysterious group of people that was bigger than a herd of wildebeest and zebra following the rain. As was inherent in the nature of their people, they decided to remain hidden and flee if necessary.

Xi wakes early the next morning. A disquiet has settled on the valley in the night and a chill runs through his bones. He rouses his brothers and they start out at a jog-trot. The dew on the grass brushes off against their legs and runs down between their toes. All is quiet, too quiet. They have covered several miles before Xi notices the thin column of smoke climbing skyward out of their valley. With a muttered click of disgust he sends his brothers on and turns back to admonish the women for their foolhardiness. He runs hard now, for the fire must be put out before the smoke is seen.

He hops across a stream, but in his haste fails to notice a foot print in the wet sand. Rounding the boulder which hides his cave, the rebuke dies on his lips, as he stares, mouthing soundless words of horror.

Six dark men fill the cave. One is standing and he towers above Xi's tiny frame. A baby lies face down in the fire, its scorched hair and flesh filling the cave with an acrid stench. Xi's woman lies in a disjointed bundle on the floor. Blood stains her kaross and her jaw lies at a crazy angle to her face. A whimper escapes from the back of the cave and in the half light he sees a man on top of a San girl – he is almost twice her size.

An arrow sings from his bow and catches the standing man full in the belly. A second arrow penetrates deep into another's thigh. He notches a third, but it skitters harmlessly off the cave roof as an assegai skewers him at the base of the throat, protruding through his back. As he falls, he sees through a mist of pain and tears that the man is still on top of the girl.

Ghanza continues to eat on a piece of kudu until Xi's

body has stopped twitching. He stands, places his foot on the tiny chest and withdraws the assegai.

"You," he says, pointing with the bloodied tip at the man on top of the girl, "go and see if there are any more of these little devils who wish to ambush us."

"But," protests the man.

Ghanza's assegai goes back, poised to throw. The man rolls off the girl, picks up his own assegai and spear and goes out of the cave.

"What of the arrows?" Ghanza asks the wounded men.

"Ha!" says the one. "They are but puny sticks that break easily – I have already pushed this one through and out." He stands holding the small arrowhead as blood flows down his leg.

"I cannot push mine through," complains the second warrior. "It has barbs and I lack the courage to pull it out myself. Pull it out for me, Ghanza."

Ghanza takes hold of the short shaft protruding from the man's belly, pulls gently, twists the shaft slightly, then pulls gently again. With a heavy jerk he rips the head free. The man sways on his feet and sweat courses down his face. Not a word escapes his lips.

Ghanza turns his attention to the girl. Her eyes are closed and a light foam flecks her lips. Three times he drives his assegai into her unconscious form.

Pity and mercy are not part of Ghanza's make-up. These and other similar emotions were disciplined out of him when he was conscripted to Shaka's army as a boy of fifteen. He had been recruited to an *impi* under General Manukosi and had grown in prestige to become one of Manukosi's lieutenants.

Manukosi, however, had become disgruntled with Shaka and he and several thousand loyal supporters, including Ghanza, had deserted and were now fleeing towards the Limpopo River.

Ghanza knelt prostrate in the dirt. "*Numzaan!*" he said.

"Lift your head and tell me why your assegai is bloodied," said Manukosi.

Ghanza told his story of the band of little people.

Prior to their encounter with Xi they had found several similar groups along their line of march and had always found these tiny folk unwilling to pierce their ears and thus signify their allegiance. They kept no cattle or grain and it had been decided to put them all to death.

"Mmm," said Manukosi, "and what of the two warriors who did not return?"

Hesitating, Ghanza glanced around the thornbush enclosure.

"You may speak," said Manukosi, "the mouths here will remain silent."

"The two men were struck by arrows from the little man's bow and although both were fairly small wounds, the men became dizzy and sick within a short march. They died within the time it takes a serpent to swallow a frog. It was the work of powerful poison."

A silence fell over the small gathering. Poison signified witchcraft and protection by the spirits.

"And what of the other matter?" asked Manukosi, more to break the uneasiness that had settled than with any other intention.

"I think that I have found a place," replied Ghanza.

"What, where?" shouted Manukosi, leaping up from the log which had formed his seat. "Ghanza, you are indeed a great lieutenant, I shall add two head of cattle to your kraal and you shall be the Master of the Hunt."

Ghanza prostrated himself again in the face of such glory.

The place which Ghanza had found was a long meandering valley. The hills on either side had been gentle at first but as the valley narrowed, they became steeper and steeper until they were almost cliff-like and the valley floor was a narrow bottleneck.

Ghanza was given a thousand men and with these he dug two pits across the narrowest part of the valley floor. The pits were so deep that a man sitting on another's shoulders could not see out of them and the edges were lined with logs so that they would not crumble. At the end of the fifth day he was ready.

As the first light of dawn streaked the sky a rough semicircle of Manukosi's followers stretched across the valley floor and up the slopes at the head of the valley. At the beat of a drum they started forward in silence. The passage of their feet through the grass carried like the whisper of a wind through a forest.

A reedbuck's head shot up from a patch of green at which it had been nibbling. The nearest man was sixty metres away and with a shrill whistle the animal fled in a series of short bounds. Slowly, more and more animals sensed the advancing human wall and started moving off down the valley.

An eland bull had just drunk his fill from a small pool when the line of figures appeared through the grass. He galloped across the valley and started up the hill. In his fright he almost ran into a flank of men; his eyes widened in terror and his nostrils flared as he turned and fled again.

The thunder of hooves now carried on the cold morning air. It was joined by a deep rumble that rolled across the valley. Ghanza felt the prickle of a thrill run down his spine as the sound reached him. It was the massed bass voices of Manukosi's men joined in song.

Manukosi sat on a rock above the pits and the song reached his ears just as the leading animal ran towards the first trench. It was an impala ewe and she jumped clear across with what seemed an effortless defiance of gravity. She misjudged the second pit, however, and crashed headlong into the far wall. She staggered to her feet and started to run up and down the pit. Manukosi slapped his thigh in delight.

An eland bull was next and without hesitation it leapt into the pit and out the other side. The second pit was just as easily overcome and cursing Manukosi hurled a long spear down at the fleeing animal. He missed, clapped his hands and praised the eland for its courage.

A press of animals now converged on the pits. A zebra galloped over the edge, its hooves flaying the air. It crashed to the bottom, splintering its leg below the knee. The animal's scream of pain and terror was lost in the thunder of hooves and voices. A cloud of dust rose above the valley. It clogged Ghanza's eyes as he advanced with the line of beaters. He blinked it away, the excitement hot and heady in his throat. To his right a jackal tried to break through the line and was laughingly lifted on the point of an assegai to be thrown forward again.

Below Manukosi the first pit was almost full and the screams of terrified and dying animals rent the air. Soon the pit filled and a wave of animals flowed into the second pit, filling it within minutes. The remaining animals fled over the bridge of bodies, escaping the slaughter.

Manukosi was ecstatic and called Ghanza to him as soon as he arrived.

"Master of the Hunt," he addressed him formally, "tonight we shall sing your praise, for our people shall eat for a long time on the meat we have gathered today." □

The moon had now risen, bathing the tree above us in pale, colourless light.

The old man, momentarily silent, was staring at the coals that had now lost their intensity. From far away a lion's roar carried to us on a gentle breeze that rustled the leaves. It seemed to pull him out of his reverie.

He rubbed his hands vigorously above the fire. "Why don't you fetch a few beers while I put some more logs on the fire?" he suggested, turning to me.

When I returned, I saw that Mbambo had joined the old man and was sitting on a sawn-off log that he had pulled close to the coals. He seemed totally unperturbed by the clouds of smoke that rose from the logs and wafted occasionally into his face.

He and the old man had the kind of friendship that is rare amongst men and comes only from a lifetime experienced alongside another. Mbambo was the elder, his sparse, slate-grey peppercorn hair and the few like-coloured wisps on his chin giving him a most dignified appearance of which he appeared to be unaware.

I handed out the beer and they both cracked the seals and drank from the cans.

The beers were half empty and the flames were flicking high above the logs before the old man continued. He spoke partly in Shangaan now as was his habit in Mbambo's presence when they continually switched between English and Shangaan.

Much happened after Ghanza's great hunt. It is said that Shaka sent an army to slaughter Manukosi and his men, but that instead of fighting each other, the two bands joined forces. Again Shaka sent out warriors, but this time they never got beyond what we now know as the Olifants River, because the men were weak from lack of food.

Years of bloodshed and war followed as Manukosi's army raided the surrounding country – some think that the area was named after those years: the 'land of much blood', Gazankulu. Eventually Manukosi reached boundary agreements with his neighbours and put an end to warmongering, but no sooner was he securely established, than he began to imagine traitors in his midst.

Over the years, Ghanza had become one of Manukosi's favourite lieutenants and now that peace reigned, their kraals lay close together. After a time, however, Ghanza noticed that Manukosi was becoming more and more cool towards him, apparently jealous of his popularity amongst the Bashangane, as the people were now called. Manukosi was convinced that some of his own men were plotting against him and already some heads had rolled.

Late one night, as Ghanza sat in a log enclosure smoking a pipe of *insangu* (marijuana) – as was his privilege as head of the kraal – a shadow detached itself from a wall. With his free hand Ghanza grasped the shaft of his short stabbing assegai.

"A life for a life," whispered the approaching figure.

Ghanza half rose, his body tensed for attack, then recognized the man – it was a warrior he had saved from an enemy's assegai some years before. He motioned the man to sit.

"Your life is in peril," said the visitor quietly, "they say you are to be killed . . . tomorrow, at first light."

Ghanza raised his assegai in a gesture of despair, then bowed his head in acceptance. "So, it has come," he said.

After a moment he looked up at his visitor. There was a silent question in his eyes.

"I can say no more," said the man. "I have paid my debt. *Hamba kahle* (go well) brother – and go swiftly."

"*Sala kahle* (stay well) brother, and thank you."

Ghanza glanced back only once as he literally ran for his life. The sun had been above the horizon for an hour and a column of smoke hung suspended in the air. He wondered if it were his kraal that was burning.

For two days he travelled without stopping, heading towards the foothills of the distant mountains and eating frugally from a stodgy lump of mealie porridge and some cooked meat. On the third day he collapsed next to a stream that cascaded down a cliff above him. When he awoke the sun had sunk low and he felt stiff and cold in the chill evening air. His assegais were gone! Not far from his head lay a small bundle and next to it was a single tiny footprint.

Expecting to feel the prick of a small arrow, he reached slowly for the bundle. But no arrow came, and in the bundle he found a few pieces of lightly cooked meat and fat and some bulbs.

For several days Ghanza travelled along the foot of the mountains and not once did he see sign that the little people had passed, yet often the base of his scalp prickled as he felt someone watching him.

Eventually he turned away from the security that the huge buttresses and dense forests had afforded him and started to follow a line of outcrops that reached into the plains below.

At the foot of one of these outcrops he found a small kraal and told the people there of the place he was seeking. The headman said that he knew of the place and although he had not been there, he thought it to be eight days' walk to the south. A week later, having asked directions from another kraal, Ghanza at last arrived at his destination.

The first thing he came upon was a field of trees laden with an orange fruit. The scent was intoxicating and he wandered aimlessly through the orchard until the sound of voices and laughter attracted him.

Unwittingly, he had walked into a garden and the scene he found stopped him dead in his tracks. A young girl clad only in a loincloth laughed as she poured water into a large tub. Inside the tub lay a man like none he had seen before. His skin was as white as the feathers of the bird that followed the cattle. His hair was black, but it was long and straight and he had a beard that hung from his face like the mane of a lion. Ghanza's jaw hung slack against his chest.

"What do you want?" growled the man. The girl had stopped laughing.

There was a sharp crack and a bullet whined above Ghanza's head. He dropped to all fours.

"*Ulawaini?*" (What do you want?) the man asked again, impatiently.

"I, I am looking for Juwawa," stammered Ghanza, looking down at the ground and trying to recover his composure.

"Well, you've found him. Now go and wait at the house," laughed the man.

Ghanza turned and moved off in the direction in which the man had pointed. The girl's shrill laugh followed him.

João Albassini or 'Juwawa', as he was known amongst the local tribes, sank back in the warm soapy water. He had some thinking to do and decisions to make.

The girl's lithe fingers glided up his arms to his hairy shoulders. She massaged the warm water over his neck and traced intricate patterns down his spine. She slipped a hand on to his chest and rubbed his nipple with the base of her palm. The hand began to gently pinch him and moved slowly down over his stomach. Her little finger began to explore his navel. He reached over and gently removed her hand.

"I'll call you in a while," he said, biting a fingertip, "but first I must think."

She pouted, swung her breasts close to his face and flounced off into the garden.

Juwawa had arrived from the coast and set himself up as a trader towards the end of 1830. Was it that long ago? he frowned to himself.

He was the first European to have settled in the area and he began trading European goods for ivory and rhino horn. Soon he began to employ his own hunters whom he armed with guns. His trips to Delagoa Bay with loads of tusks and horns became more frequent. He built himself a homestead of brick with fine gardens and orchards, and a large storeroom for the tusks.

His band of hunters grew. They were refugees from different tribes, like the one who had arrived this morning, seeking a haven behind the security of his rifles, and with their assistance tusks and horns had been gathered in ever increasing numbers.

How long had it been before he decided to move further south? Eight, nine years? No, it was more like ten. His band had stayed with him and defeated the people of Siluvane, with whom he then settled.

For years his tusk trade flourished but suddenly it began to falter. He employed more hunters, but still fewer tusks came in and his store had not seen a rhino horn for three years.

He had temporarily moved back to his original camp, hoping to cover a wider area, but in three months only two pairs of tusks had passed through his hands. This morning his head huntsman had arrived back after a month and a half without having seen an elephant track.

Had the time come for João Albassini to move back to the coast?

"Yes, I think so," he said to himself, "but," he smiled at the sky, "I shall have the last hunt."

He whistled softly. The girl appeared through the trees, her eyes shining with excitement. She dunked her hands into the water and leant over the tub, then shrieked as he pulled her in with him. The gardener peered at them in astonishment through a shrub as the water splashed and slopped. The tub wobbled, teetered precariously and eventually fell over, spilling its contents on the lawn. □

The old man's description of this scene was somewhat more detailed and colourful than it stands here, but the subtleties of Shangaan idiom do not easily lend themselves to direct translation.

Mbambo rocked back and forth on his log in silent mirth. He poured the last of his beer into his mouth where it mingled with the laughter in his throat and made him choke.

Spluttering, he stood up, waved his hand in farewell to his friend and walked stiffly into the night. The old man's only acknowledgment of Mbambo's departure was to switch back to English.

"Hey, Dad, come and look at this!"

"What's it, Hennie?"

"It looks like an old bath, I wonder what it's doing just lying here in the veld?"

"I don't know, but I just found the ruins of a brick house up there, and those appear to be orange trees," said Jan de Lange, pointing at some trees beyond a small thicket of acacias.

"I wonder if this was Albassini's home," said Hennie. "It could be. They say it was because of him that there are no elephant or rhino here now. Anyway, it seems like a pleasant spot. We'll make camp here."

Axes and pangas flew to work and the small stand of thorn trees in front of the orange grove disappeared. Within an hour, the entourage of black men who accompanied Jan de Lange and his eldest son on their hunting trips had erected a stout circular barricade of thorns.

The horses were led into the confines of the barricade, the De Langes' tent was erected and the blacks cleared themselves an area for sleeping. Several fires were lit and large quantities of wood were brought in from the surrounding veld.

The dark cloak of a moonless night settled upon them. Jan de Lange's mouth watered, as the aroma of wildebeest kidneys roasting on the coals filled the night air.

They had not yet begun to eat when a throaty growl rumbled through their conversation. The incessant chatter that issued from around the blacks' cooking fire

ceased abruptly. They piled wood on to the perimeter fires until the flames licked high into the night sky, briefly scaring the darkness back a few metres.

"Another night with the damnable lions bothering us," sighed De Lange. "Those poor fellows won't sleep a wink again," he said, inclining his head towards the blacks.

The lion growled again, closer this time. Jan grabbed his revolver and fired three shots in the direction of the growl. The last shot ricocheted off something solid and whined away into the night. The blacks, satisfied that the danger had at least been temporarily removed, took up their chatter where they had left off.

"I wonder why the lions always seem to bother us at night?" asked Hennie.

"Well, we keep the horses in the enclosure and there is no doubt that lions are fond of horseflesh."

"*Ja*! I suppose it could also be the smell of all the meat."

"That too,"agreed his father.

"Why don't they rather hunt wild animals?" asked Hennie in exasperation.

"Well, this would appear to be easier pickings and anyway, as we have seen, there are not that many wild animals left here any more. We won't make enough biltong to sell this year and we haven't even got a single giraffe hide.

"Did there really used to be that much more game than there is now?" asked Hennie.

"Ha!" laughed his father. "More? This land was teeming with animals, it was a hunter's paradise. When I first came down here in '71 I bagged thirty giraffe and three wagonloads of biltong – now those were the good old days! The highveld game was not breeding fast enough and there was nothing left to shoot, so we came down to the lowveld. Those first years were by far the best. But then the farmers started bringing their sheep and cattle down for winter grazing and the game disappeared from the foothills of the mountains. Then they opened that highway from Lydenburg to Delagoa Bay and any '*Jan Rap en sy maat*' who had a rifle came down here to shoot." Jan de Lange shook his head in agitation.

"But what about all the natives that Abel Erasmus had removed?" asked Hennie.

"*Ja*, well we knew that that was a major problem," said Jan. "The natives would live here in the unhealthy months and during that time would poach as much as they could. Then when we came down in the winter, there was less and less game every year. Old Abel was Native Commissioner at that time and was a hunter himself, so he understood the problem. When we boers petitioned him to do something about it, that morning after the long '*kerkdiens*', he went straight to work. In a short

time he had removed the natives from this area and re-settled them elsewhere with their stock and belongings. But the native is a funny being, and in no time at all most of them had run away. Some came back here and others went to Mozambique."

"Well, if there's not that much game left here, why don't we hunt further east or north?" asked Hennie.

"Two reasons," said his father. "Firstly, we can't take the horses in there because of the tsetse fly. Its bite gives them sleeping sickness and they would all die. Secondly, because there are a lot of natives up north and they poach and still have drives where they chase the game into pits." Hennie started to speak but his father held up his hand to stop him. Draining the last of the coffee from his mug he stood up.

"Now you have made me tired with all this talking, I am turning in. Good night."

During the night, Jan de Lange woke to hear the lion growling. It did not disturb him unduly so he rolled over and soon fell asleep again. An hour later, he woke to pandemonium. Shouts and screams from the blacks mixed with the terrified whinnies and snorts of the horses. "*Nkosaan, Nkosaan, ingonyama!*" (Sir, sir, lion!) he heard Jacob shout.

A horse barged into the side of the tent in its terror, half collapsing it. The terrified animal's hooves pounded hard into Jan's belly and he threw an arm up to protect his face. A hoof caught him a glancing blow on the throat and he choked and retched, sending spasms of pain through his torso. Another hoof landed beside him and then the horse was gone.

Hennie struggled out from under the restraining canvas clutching his rifle. He blinked rapidly as his eyes adjusted to the light of the blazing fires. The blacks were all huddled in the far corner and one howled in pain as he tried to push his way through the barrier of thorns. Only one horse had not broken its line and it stood now, nostrils flared and eyes wide with fear. Another ran back and forth behind the tent. Two were gone.

A lioness stood over the carcass of the wildebeest they had shot that morning. Her amber eyes glinted in the light and her tail slashed from side to side. She turned her head towards him as her growl chilled the air. Her eyes bored right through him and Hennie felt the hair on his arms and legs prickle erect.

Slowly, ever so slowly, he lifted the rifle. The sights came up and found a spot between her eyes. The barrel shook slightly. He squeezed the trigger.

Click! Hennie froze. "Idiot," he cursed.

The lioness returned her attention to the wildebeest, slowly dragging it towards the perimeter of thorns. With hands drenched in sweat and starting to shake uncon-

trollably, Hennie searched his pockets. He found a single round in his trousers. Thumbing it into the breech, he knelt and lifted the rifle again.

As the lioness's head was hidden behind the wildebeest, it would have to be a heart or lung shot. Again he took aim. The barrel shook dangerously. The rifle barked and kicked back into his shoulder. With an angry snarl the lioness dropped the wildebeest and turned as Hennie stood up. With two swift bounds she charged and leapt into the air. Hennie grabbed his rifle by the barrel and lashed out at her, striking her square on the shoulder. The butt splintered and broke. The lioness crashed into him, knocking him backwards and pinning him beneath her. He screamed, hysteria swamping his senses, his voice jumping an octave in terror. Tears rolled down his cheeks and he felt his bladder release, soaking his pants and running warm down his crotch.

The lioness slid off him slightly. He lay still for a full ten seconds before he realized that she was dead.

It took an hour and a half before order was restored to their camp. They would have to look for the two missing horses in the morning. Hennie sat staring into the fire, sipping coffee. Slowly his body stopped shaking but he remained by the fire's warmth until dawn. Now silent, now having sporadic conversation, as his father, still in pain, offered him comfort and praise.

Jan de Lange decided that it was time that he and his party turned back. They would return to their wagons. It would take time to bring in all the cattle and there was still the long slow drive, at an ox's walking pace, back to Lydenburg.

When all was packed and ready, Jan de Lange called his *induna* to him.

"Jacob," he said, "I want someone to go after those two horses and bring them back to the wagons. If they are dead or die along the way he is to skin them and bring the skins back with him. Here is a rifle and twenty rounds."

"*Yebo, Nkosaan,*" said Jacob. "I'll send Nagmaal."

Jan de Lange grinned to himself and nodded. That name had always amused him – imagine calling your child "communion".

Nagmaal was big for a Shangaan and although he looked somewhat fat, was unusually powerful. He had been named Hathlawe Ngobeni but had adopted 'Nagmaal' when he sought employment, for the convenience of his employer whose inexpert tongue would not have been able to deal with 'Hathlawe'.

Having received the rifle and his instructions, Hathlawe set off on the trail of the horses. His heart thumped with excitement; he could not believe his luck. This was even more than he had wished for.

The tracks showed that the horses had been pursued by two other lions, which had soon given up the chase. The horses had run hard for quite a distance, but had eventually slowed to a walk and, as he expected, had turned and headed towards the wagons.

On the second day Hathlawe found what he was looking for. The horses had passed fairly close to a small group of huts. Approaching them, he found an old man and woman and enquired after the horses. Then, satisfied that his visit would be remembered, he set out on the tracks again.

He continued to follow the horses for a short distance to the northwest. Then, with a smile, he left the tracks and turned south. There was a lightness to his step and he caressed the rifle. It was now his.

Hathlawe had heard that a lot of money was to be earned in the south, where the white man was laying long lines of steel through the wilderness for the *stimela* (steam train).

He found the railhead after wandering for several weeks through the bush. Carefully wrapping the rifle in a cloth soaked in fat, as he had seen Jan de Lange do, he buried it and set out to find employment.

Hathlawe found himself standing in front of a small table under an umbrella thorn.

"What's your name, boy?" asked the man seated at the table, addressing him as he addressed all blacks irrespective of age. Hathlawe stared uncomprehendingly at the ground.

"Your bloody *gama!*" shouted the small Scot, his red beard flashing with the movement of his jaw.

"Uh! Uh! Tymon," said Hathlawe, realizing that the man was not Afrikaans-speaking and therefore 'Nagmaal' would not be acceptable.

"That's a new one," muttered the Scot to himself. "All right, *hamba* bloody joba!" he shouted at the newly christened Tymon.

Tymon turned and headed towards a gang of blacks who were busy excavating a cut through a small undulation in the ground. An empty bottle crashed on a rock next to him. "Hurry up, you lazy slob!" There was a pop as a cork was removed from a fresh bottle.

"*Sakubona.*" (I see you.)

"*Sakubona,*" came the reply.

"How are you?"

"No, I am well. How are you?"

"I too am well but for the foul taste of the 'one with hair of fire' in my mouth," said Tymon and spat.

"Yes, we call him Tongue of Fire," replied the man, and he too spat. "I am called Elmon," he said and extended his hand.

"Tymon," he said, clasping the proffered hand, then releasing it and clasping the thumb, releasing that and re-clasping the hand.

Just then a wagon rolled into view moving slowly towards them.

"Come," said Elmon, "we need someone strong like you to help off-load."

"What is it?" asked Tymon.

"Our weekly meat ration."

"A whole wagonload per week for less than fifty people?" Tymon asked in surprise.

"You will learn," said Elmon. "Most of it rots and is thrown away – you see, Tongue of Fire pays the hunter for the weight of the meat that he brings in, but before he pays him he takes some of the payment for himself."

The wagon drew up and the coloured hunter climbed down and accepted a glass of yellow-brown liquor from Tongue of Fire. Tymon began to unload and his eyes widened in astonishment as he off-loaded, amongst other things, a baby vervet monkey, a crocodile and an old male baboon. He even found seven terrapins that surely only the maggots would eat.

The months that ensued were a blur of misery, pain and abuse, but Tymon stayed on. The money was good and the more Tongue of Fire maltreated him, the stronger burnt the desire for revenge in his chest.

People fell sick around him; malaria, dysentery and cholera made skeletons of men and many died. Their bodies were dragged into the bush and the growls and whoops of the ever present lions and hyaenas were their final blessing.

Healthy and strong as he was Tymon did not escape entirely and fell ill with dysentery, but he managed to ward it off by drinking a brew made from the umPhafa tree (buffalo-thorn). One day as he squatted in his misery in the bush, Tongue of Fire by chance found him. "Ha! I knew that's what you were made of," he laughed, and spat a stream of yellow liquid which caught Tymon on the knee and slipped down his shin.

On another occasion Tymon was instructed to move Tongue of Fire's table and while doing so stumbled, spilling a cup of tea which contained mostly spirits. The Scot had stood up on his toes and the flat of his hand at full swing caught the side of Tymon's head, spinning it around. Tymon's knuckles showed white through his skin as he put the table down and, silently drawing on all his self-control, turned and went back to work. Elmon had put a hand of friendship on his back.

On Tymon's arrival, Tongue of Fire had selected him to accompany Elmon on the biweekly trip to collect the wages because he was "a big strong kaffir!" They were aware that Tongue of Fire drew wages for sixty blacks,

when on average he had only about forty working in his gang – the difference swelled his coffers. The pay office was about fifty-five kilometres back down the track, which required a four-day trip there and back.

When Elmon and Tymon were on their way back from one trip and had stopped for the night, Tymon chastised and teased Elmon until he agreed to open the metal box that contained the wages by holding it over the fire. They had long ago worked out how to open and close the box without breaking the seal, but this time was to be different.

The seal came away. They ignored the smaller envelopes and drew out the one marked "Advance Gang Supervisor". A tin of water boiled on the fire. The lip of the envelope was held above it and soon wrinkled open. They emptied the contents on to a cloth between them.

In the silence, their anger grew as they saw for the first time that Tongue of Fire was paid more than the whole gang combined.

Tymon began to talk, formulating a plan. Elmon, reluctant at first, grew excited and soon agreed. They arrived back at their camp late the following afternoon. Immediately after darkness had settled, a hushed council with all the blacks was held. Without a single objection voiced, a unanimous oath to secrecy was sworn.

Later, as a midnight moon crept into a blackened sky, two figures stole through a narrow gap in the perimeter of thorns and approached Tongue of Fire's tent.

In the morning, the tent, the perimeter fence, the table and any sign that a red-headed Scotsman had once existed had gone.

Work continued as usual, and the hunter was told that Tongue of Fire had gone temporarily. He was paid for the meat, less the usual commission. Biweekly the wages were collected as before and the now large excess divided evenly between the 'advance gang'.

For four months all went well. Then as the following payday approached, word flashed down the line that there were no wages. In three hours along seventy miles of track the sound of tools at work died away.

To try to explain bankruptcy was too difficult; there was just 'no money'.

Hathlawe built himself a hut not far from the railhead. One day, walking aimlessly down the deserted track, he found a trolley and manhandled it back on to the rails. For several years he provided for himself and then managed to adequately support a wife and family by shooting animals, loading them on the trolley and poling it seventy miles to Komatipoort.

One year a great many animals died. The stench of rotting flesh hung in a pungent mantle over the veld. Vultures adorned dead trees, their pendulant bellies weigh-

ing them with discomfort. At night the whoop and maniacal cackle of the hyaenas resounded as they sat to the banquet. The massive *inyathi* (buffalo) appeared to have gone for ever. Hathlawe was also told by several passing travellers that to the north and east the tsetse fly had fled the death that lay everywhere. When he had told the man who bought his meat of the great die-off, he had merely nodded and said, "*Ja!* The rinderpest."

Here the old man paused in his story to open a fresh beer. He lit the pipe that had lain forgotten in his hand and continued.

"Wave at the old man, darling!" the young woman encouraged.

The child shyly raised his hand, opening and closing his fingers. The old black man beyond the window stared impassively back. His hair was grizzled and his skin hung from what must once have been an impressive frame.

Hathlawe sat on a wooden stool in front of his hut. He saw the hand raised in greeting but it did not register; his eyes were fixed on the child's mop of red hair.

The image blurred and Hathlawe slipped into another of his daydreams. In 1899 the white men had made war on each other and his trolley had been taken from him. His rifle, however, had remained hidden.

Twice their *impi* had come down the track. There had been much shooting but it was all at animals. They seemed to take great delight in killing, for many of the carcasses were left lying in the veld. They soon tired of the sport, however, and went back the way they had come.

A son of Hathlawe's wife's clan arrived one day and told them that the war had ended. The area that they lived in had now been set aside as a reserve for the wild animals. The import of this did not reach Hathlawe until the visitor told him that he would have to surrender his rifle. "My son," Hathlawe had said, "the enthusiasm of youth has clouded your judgement. You cannot take my rifle from me."

Two weeks later, the young man arrived back with several other 'guards of the game', as they called themselves, and a white man. Bewildered and filled with resentment, Hathlawe had handed over his rifle, his companion of years and provider for his family. His small clan turned to snaring to obtain their meat.

Years of quiet again enveloped his life where the only excitement was the occasional visit of a guard. A frenzy of activity would follow the announcement of his approach, as all meat was hurriedly hidden.

Then the men had come back and started work on the

rails again. Hathlawe and his sons worked on the railway for three years, until its completion.

A succession of loud clacks invaded Hathlawe's thoughts. The red image in front of him jolted. He came out of his reverie as the train started to move.

"*Hau*," he thought, "this is the third train this week. Many more than when they first began."

The child still waved uncertainly as the carriage drew away. "Perhaps he cannot see too well, darling," said the woman, putting a consoling arm around her child's shoulders. She had been unnerved by the black man's fixed stare and was happy to be leaving him behind.

The conductor tapped on the glass pane of the compartment door and opened it slightly.

"Your siding next, Mrs Burke," he said. "I'll send someone for your bags."

Mrs Burke nodded and smiled. "Thank you," she said.

Her compartment companion with the child looked startled. "This is where you live? I thought that you were on a pleasure trip to view the animals."

"No, dear," replied the older woman, "my husband works a cattle ranch out here." She saw the veiled admiration grow in the young woman's eyes.

A horsedrawn buggy awaited Mrs Burke. She smiled to herself as passengers on the train stared in disbelief as she trotted her horses down a track into the bush.

"Grace!" her husband boomed as he strode from the stoep of the house. His huge calloused hands lifted her without effort from the seat of the buggy. He kissed her lightly. "I missed you," he said, looking into her eyes.

She felt his warm strength fill the emptiness that had been with her all the while she had been away.

"Agnes has just made the tea."

"Oh! Good, that's just what I need," she said, collapsing beside him on to the *riempie* bench on the stoep.

They sat in silence, enjoying each other's presence.

"Oh, it's so good to be back!" she said, taking the tray from Agnes and thanking her. "Johannesburg has just grown out of all proportion. The streets are filled with more motor vehicles than trams and everything is so rushed and noisy. I see that there was a fire while I was away," she said, changing the subject.

"Mmm!" he said, sipping his tea. "It swept through most of the western section. We should have good grass there in a month or two."

"And the cattle?" she asked.

"I've moved them over to the east for the moment," he said slowly, knowing what her next question would be.

"Lions?"

"Yes," he replied, "they're still fairly numerous in that area. They've already taken a few head."

"You cannot possibly go out hunting the first night I get back," she said, placing both her hands on his thigh. She loathed those nights alone in the house. She would toss and turn, unable to sleep. She had taken to reading to stop the thought of him alone in the bush with the lions from taunting her. He had shot several hundred already and each time he went out it was worse for her.

"No, no!" he said, patting her hand, "I'll not go out for a few days yet."

It was his turn to change the subject. "A few farms were sold while you were away."

She stared at him wide-eyed.

"Mmm!" he said, teasing her.

"We're going to have neighbours?" she asked, her delight obvious.

"Unfortunately, I do not think that the new owners will live here permanently," he replied, "It would appear that they want to leave the farms as an undeveloped wilderness, using them for hunting and holidays."

"Perhaps they'll shoot the lions for you," she said, slumping back in disappointment.

He smiled softly and put his arm around her.

Two days later Fredrick Burke set out. A herdsman had reported one of his cattle killed by lions that morning and only a little of the carcass had been eaten. The lions would certainly be back again that night.

The herdsman led him to a spot just beyond a dry stream where a mottled orange and white ox lay stifflegged in the afternoon sun. Its stomach cavity was a gaping hole. The situation was ideal. The herdsman slashed the grass around the carcass and chopped down a small rain tree that would have obscured Burke's vision.

He gave the herdsman his horse with instructions to return after the sun had risen. Climbing a marula tree, he settled down to wait.

He was lucky, this marula had some thick branches, several of which provided sturdy forks into which he could wedge himself. His jacket hung askew, pulled down by the weight of cartridges in the pocket. He tied a bag with a bottle of cold tea and some sandwiches against the trunk.

The darkness began to filter down through the trees. A scops owl started to call, the short rolling note repeated so regularly you could almost set your watch by it. The grass below him rustled slightly and parted. A small genet padded forward across the area of slashed grass. It paused beside the carcass. "I don't think you're responsible," he thought, smiling to himself. The tiny creature had heard something. It stood now in a comical stance on its back legs with its forepaws held against its chest. The bulky carcass still obscured its vision but its ears moved back and forth, searching for a sound. Sud-

23

denly it bounded away in long elastic strides, scampering into the undergrowth.

A tawny form emerged from the enclosing darkness. With a deep sigh it collapsed and started licking its paws. Two more arrived. One bent down and ran its head along the prone lion's shoulders and neck. They approached the carcass and pawed it, their sharp claws digging into the flesh. A large lioness appeared, bringing five sub-adults with her. The youngsters played and cavorted, hiding between tufts of grass and behind the carcass. One came fairly close to the marula in which Burke sat hidden. He froze.

It failed to sense him and went back to join the others who had started to feed.

He bided his time for about half an hour. By then twelve lions were growling and fighting over the carcass. The large female who had arrived first still lay off to the side and next to her lay a large male whose mane was not yet fully developed. It was the male he chose first.

It lay with its eyes closed, its head on the ground. Slowly he aimed his rifle at it in the darkness. He snapped on the torch. Light flooded the scene. Quickly the centre of the beam found the sleeping male. A lion at the carcass growled. The male started to lift his head, blinking. The rifle spat a short tongue of flame. The lions scattered in panic. The male's head fell back and his legs kicked spasmodically at the grass. Soon he lay still. The torch went off.

The others, seeing the male lying at the carcass, overcame their fright and slowly came back to feed. Only one bothered to sniff the dead male.

Burke repeated the process again and again. At two in the morning the lions stopped returning to the carcass. Eight lions lay dead. He wedged himself against the tree and dozed until a pink-tinged cloud announced dawn.

On his way home he rode past the newly planted cotton fields, with their rows of budding green plants stretching around the hill. He reined in his horse. Climbing down, he walked along between the rows. Little puffs of dust rose up from his heels. Every now and then he bent down and muttered to himself. The kudu and duiker were taking their toll of the little plants. He headed back to his horse. It had been the same with the mealies but now they were doing very well. He mounted, lit his pipe and let the horse make its own way home.

Grace was pushing the new pale blue perambulator around the yard as he approached down a wagon sled track from the east. She laughed, embarrassed, as she saw him. "I just couldn't resist getting a bit of practice."

"You have a way to go," he said, glancing down at her slightly bulging belly. "Don't wear it out before he

arrives!" He bent over in the saddle and kissed the top of her head. ☐

The old man's voice had grown very quiet as he related this part of the story. The pace at which he was talking had also slowed considerably. The story at this point was very close to the bone.

I pushed the logs deeper into the fire with the tip of my boot. The old man took the opportunity to pause, and blew his nose loudly into an enormous handkerchief before continuing.

☐ "Why, Dad?"
Young David Burke watched, bewildered, as the last of his father's cattle were herded on to the trucks at the railway siding.

Fredrick Burke reached down and affectionately tousled his son's hair. He squatted on his haunches beside the boy.

"As you know, David, many of the farms around here are being sold to people who want to keep them as a natural wilderness. The company that owns our farm has decided to sell it too because it will realize a good profit from the land and cattle."

"Does that mean we have to leave the bush?"

Fredrick Burke lifted his eyes to the horizon and just squeezed his son's shoulder in reply.

At ten years old David Burke did not understand the pain in his father's eyes. ☐

The old man was quiet for a long time. He mumbled something to himself and began tapping his pipe out on his chair leg. His tale was complete.

I knew him well enough to know that he would not discuss its subtleties with me, preferring that I explore them on my own and draw my own conclusions. It was strange that we could come so close to the heart and yet would not reach out and touch it. The act would be too brutal, it would shatter the bond.

I watched him now with his head tilted back, viewing the stars from under the tattered brim of his hat. He puffed contemplatively on his pipe.

I turned my attention back to the fire and sipped my long-forgotten drink. I thought of the last line of his story, which had struck a chord so deep inside me.

☐ ☐ ☐ ☐ ☐

I have tried many times to put a single word to the attraction that a wilderness has for me. I have failed. It is not love, for love is too emotional. The attraction is more platonic. It has the comfort of a longstanding friendship;

I am at ease and happy in it. I do not suffer pains of separation, but in my absence from it experience a yearning to return.

Upon my return I am filled with an all-pervading sense of peace. It is harsh, but strangely comforting in its harshness. It is stark but possesses a unique beauty in its lack of adornment. I find a oneness and a sense of freedom that I do not experience anywhere else.

There are many who know of what I write. For centuries man has been attracted to the wilderness. The nature of his passing has varied from being an integral part of the make-up of that wilderness to being the sole reason for its wanton destruction.

Today, on the whole, man has accepted the role of guardian and protector. Individuals have come together to ensure a constitution which recognizes the obligation to conserve and preserve. A nation has taken wild, untouched places and declared them a heritage. There are those who argue that this is sufficient and that from there onward nature should be allowed to follow its own course. This is both naïve and uninformed. By the very declaration of a reserve with a boundary, man has interfered with nature and created an imbalance.

It is often difficult to envisage the world as being different from what we have always known it to be. Standing on the edge of the escarpment looking down on the lowveld, it requires a leap of the imagination to remove the tobacco sheds, banana plantations and tarred roads from your mind's eye. But then the hills become rolling grasslands dotted with flat-topped acacias and Xi, the San, runs through the grass on a crisp, clear morning.

We have never known it like that; it is beyond our experience. I have on many occasions sat beside a fire with men of the wilderness who have watched the changes of this century. Even allowing for the eloquent waxing and exaggeration of old memories, the changes are vast. Perhaps the one that has had the most repercussions is the erection of fences.

For many years after the institution of the reserves, their boundaries were only demarcated by surveyors' beacons. With a progressive increase in agriculture and the allocation of tribal trustlands, the lowveld and its reserves came under the pressure of increasing human presence. Eventually it became necessary to fence the reserves to keep the protected in and the unwanted out.

A steel upright, a few strands of wire strung taut; by human standards a fence is an unimposing structure. To man, it is a minor hindrance – a short pause, a quick stoop and he passes on, the fence and its consequences forgotten.

To an animal, the fence is the end of its range, a solid line across a hill or open plain which it may not trans-

gress. It may seem a harsh imposition on man's part but the old adage 'one has sometimes to be cruel, to be kind' applies. If an animal were to wander beyond the bounds of its sanctuary today, its flesh would soon find its way to the pots of the hungry or its skin to the floor of those whose property, however meagre, it damaged.

Fences are the same from the outside, looking in. They keep agriculture excluded and domestic animals from entering a wilderness where they would undoubtedly encounter the same treatment as a wild animal outside the reserve. They also control the amount of human pressure a reserve experiences.

Fencing, therefore, is a necessary evil, but evil it is. By fencing a wilderness, man has made dams and lakes out of a sea. He has imposed a boundary where no boundary existed. He has upset the balance of nature and the consequences must rest on his shoulders.

There are fences that transcend even these evils. These are the fences between the reserves, where a fence has wilderness on either side of it. I have sought high and low for justification for their existence, and have found none. They are monuments to man's greed and his scepticism.

The only argument that appears valid is that of the Kruger National Park in support of their western boundary fence. It is a veterinary cordon fence, mainly to prevent the spread of foot-and-mouth and corridor diseases, which have drastic effects on domestic stock. In the Kruger National Park these diseases are endemic, whereas the private reserves are considered to be disease-free. The latter therefore form an effective buffer zone between the domestic stock on their boundaries and the diseases in the Park. The fence, then, is there to contain the disease.

Even with this justification, the western boundary fence of the Kruger Park has been erected at a great cost, other than monetary, for it has cut across a wildebeest migration route. In its first year of existence, thousands of wildebeest battered themselves to death against it. This spectacle may be difficult to envisage, but try counting to a thousand and when you tire, remember that each number is an animal suffering a cruel and painful death.

The wildebeest population crashed and today, although numbers have increased, there are only small sedentary populations to remind us of the great herds that once must have been awesome to behold. Perhaps it is too much to hope that the wildebeest will migrate again, but we will never know while this fence through a wilderness exists.

By removing the fences between the reserves, we would greatly increase the sizes of our wilderness areas,

and it is obvious that the larger a wilderness is, the more 'natural' it is. The direct implications of a perimeter fence also decrease with the increased size of a reserve.

In the Kruger National Park, the sheer magnitude of the reserve allows nature to proceed, with man's presence and influence creating comparatively small disturbances. As a result, a policy of minimum management is followed, with man exercising only slight control.

The same is not true of the group of reserves on the western boundary of the Park. These reserves are comparatively much smaller than their neighbour. Most are completely fenced and experience a much higher intensity of human presence and pressure.

Through time, these factors have resulted in the smaller reserves requiring maximum management.

They are by no means unique and many of the dilemmas that they face reflect the principles and thinking of modern conservation throughout the world.

Perhaps the most fundamental requirement of any reserve is its vegetation, the source of food around which a wilderness revolves. It is the basis from which all conservation concepts must grow and to which all conservation principles must return.

To manage a reserve, man must manage the vegetation. This may sound a simple task, but remember that one does not wish to introduce artificial methods, for it is desirable to stay as close to nature's path as possible. Stop then, and consider which facets of nature we could use. There are not many – in fact there are only two: fire and water.

I do not think that there is anybody who truly knows exactly when to use fire. It is obvious when it is desperately necessary, and it is obvious, too, when its use has been a mistake. The grey area of timing between these two parameters has been argued back and forth for decades by both conservationists and farmers. The problem is that one is gambling with nature's cycles and these are fickle, to say the least.

Fire burns, but what purpose does it serve? I learnt about fire on my hands and knees.

"Well, it's no good standing up," my grey-haired mentor told me, his battered hat warding off a fierce February sun, "it only happens on the ground and a few feet above it, so that's where you have to look."

We began the exercise in a recently burned firebreak. Clouds of fine black particles rose up around me as I crawled forward on all fours and the sharp spikes of the burnt tufts made the going uncomfortable.

Through the blackened stubble little lime-green leaves pushed their way into the sunlight. Here and there the surface of the ground lay cracked and parted as young shoots broke loose from the restraint of the soil.

We came to the edge of the burn and a tangle of grass confronted me at eye level. Like a pair of high-stepping locusts, we made our way into the tangle of stalks and leaves. We had not gone five metres when we ran into a nest of pepper ticks which ended the experiment abruptly and sent us, slapping at our arms and tearing at our clothes, back to the firebreak.

As the pandemonium died down the old man asked me what I had learnt from the experiment.

"That there are ticks in long grass," I replied caustically. He smiled in agreement and pointed out that fire did control insects such as ticks but would not kill them all, because at the approach of fire ticks drop to the ground and dig themselves in, emerging once the fire has passed.

Squatting on his haunches, he pointed out what I had seen but not digested. The grass in the firebreak had been burned right down to the tuft, giving the new green leaves no competition as they emerged. Sunlight was able to reach these leaves and the ground, stimulating the roots and the leaf growth. Dormant seeds were also stimulated and fresh young plants and grasses were emerging between the tufts. He compared this with the thick mat of grass on the edge of the firebreak.

Here and there a new leaf struggled up to the sunlight between the dead stalks and leaves of previous years. He pointed out how difficult it would be for an animal to eat these new leaves between their dead predecessors. Looking below the tangle, we found no new grasses or plants emerging. Even if we had, their chances of survival would not be good as they would be conceived in the darkness and would have to push their way through the dead layer above them to reach the sun.

So to remove the layers of dead vegetation and allow sunlight through to stimulate growth of old and new grasses and plants, fire was the answer. When to use it remains a guess. Perhaps today it is more of an educated guess, but it is a guess nonetheless.

The implications of water, on the other hand, are more easily understood. Although it has been proved that some species of mammal can survive for extended periods without water, it can be accepted that where there is water you will find animals, and as that water dries up, so the animals will move away.

The practical application of this in a reserve is a relatively simple matter. Pump a waterhole and animals will move into the area; let it dry up and they will move out. This allows control of the amount of grazing and browsing that the vegetation has to withstand. Before the establishment of reserves, this type of animal movement occurred naturally as they utilized and depleted available surface water or followed localized rain storms.

In theory, the use of water should be straightforward but there are a number of complications. The largest stumbling block, strangely enough, is perennial rivers, providing a permanent natural source of water. This, however, must be accepted as a natural phenomenon; of greater importance is interference by man.

The human race has always been attracted to water – even as children, we try to dam and store it. An expanse of water, whether it is a pond or a lake, is a place of serenity and intrigue, especially in a wilderness.

As the twentieth century progressed and man gradually moved away from his position as hunter and took a new stand as protector and conservator, he began to make 'improvements' for the animals. Many of these took the form of dams and waterholes and man felt good, for his creation improved the lot of animals and provided him with visual enjoyment and satisfaction.

Permanent water introduces drastic change to a wilderness. Animals are no longer forced to move; they can become sedentary in an area of preferred grazing or browsing, eating only selected species. The animals begin to compete with each other for food and often one species will increase to the detriment of another. The composition of the vegetation changes, in some instances drastically, as particular species of grass, plant and tree are eaten year round while others remain virtually untouched. Often the habitat changes so completely that a species of mammal originally found in an area becomes locally extinct, while another, initially only present in small numbers, becomes predominant.

After fencing, permanent water probably makes the most profound contribution to the imbalance of nature, but it takes strength to admit a mistake and a gesture of complete selflessness to destroy one's creation.

There are many problems that face those who manage a wilderness, but perhaps the most difficult to deal with is intangible: an emotion. Sentimentality is an emotion that binds people and animals. It is man's empathy with something that has a right to live and his sympathy for any misery or injustice that a creature might suffer. It is ingrained in most by a society that teaches peace and pacifism and is often an instinctive reaction.

Such emotional involvement can introduce difficulties in the management of a reserve. Generally it does not, but on occasions one's judgement may be clouded, particularly regarding emotionally sensitive issues.

The best example is culling. I have run the gauntlet for my stand on culling on numerous occasions and have faced reactions ranging from righteous indignation through to bitter vehemence. To understand culling, one must rise above emotional involvement and view the argument with objectivity.

Let us remember that man created the reserves by fencing the wilderness and thereafter imposed various influences on those reserves. Generally these influences are to the direct benefit of the animal. If we consider a reserve objectively, we will see that what has been created is a sanctuary where animals can live, breed and multiply. The same is true of a herd of cows in a fenced field on a farm or, to take it one step further, a pair of mice placed in a shoe box with cotton wool, food and water. What happens is that the mice breed. Presuming that the amount of cotton wool, food and water stays the same, there will be slightly less for each mouse. Again the mice will breed and soon there will be too many to survive with the resources available in the box. The same applies to a reserve. If two or three animal species were allowed to increase to the point where the vegetation of the reserve could no longer support them, the last of the vegetation would disappear and there would be a mass death of the animals. Their numbers would crash, far below that of a normal stable population. At the same time, many different species whose numbers had not been in excess would also suffer severe losses as a result of the lack of food.

Several years after I first became involved in the wilderness, I was working in a reserve when the summer rains did not arrive. The reserve was overstocked and as the drought hardened the animals became walking skeletons and started to die. I recall one morning in particular, very vividly.

I was out walking, clad only in a pair of shorts and leather sandals. My rifle strap chafed my shoulder. The sun beat down mercilessly from a cloudless sky. The trees stood listless and scorched, their branches etched black against the azure heavens. Here and there a handful of leaves still remained to face the wrath of nature.

Not a blade of grass existed; only a few spikes of dusty, dead tufts protruded above the baked surface. Little clouds of dust rose around my feet as I made my way through this desolation.

The air was so hot and still that I felt that I could have cut it with a knife and forced it into my mouth. The sweat coursed freely down my body. Feeling drained and light-headed I eventually reached my destination, a pan that was fed by a natural spring.

The spring had dried up months before. What was once a large natural pan was now a quagmire of oozing grey-black mud, churned into a variety of strange shapes by the animals that had forced their way through it to drink the last of the water. A few hoof prints still contained a filthy mixture of mud and water.

I was about to turn away when a slight movement caught my eye. Fifteen metres away, a young impala lifted its head and bleated. It was completely covered in mud and lay splayed out in a patch of black ooze.

Shedding my sandals, I walked into the mud towards it. Its ribs and backbone showed through its skin in harsh ridged lines. It snorted ineffectually at the mud that clogged its nose and mouth. As I approached, it struggled feebly to free itself from the embrace of the cloying, sticky sludge. Its right front leg thrashed at the mud. The leg was broken and the bottom half flapped uselessly, attached only by the skin. Sharp shards and needles of bone protruded through the skin, patches of ivory in the blackness. Around its right shoulder, the mud was stained red-brown with blood. Its large brown eyes stared unblinking at me as a droplet of mud slid over one of the eyeballs.

There are few who would deny that my bullet was one of mercy. With this illustration I have merely touched the tip of an iceberg. Many hundreds of animals died that year. The vultures crowded the taller trees with distended bellies. Hyaenas and jackals ate only the choicest portions from the fallen, some of whom were still alive, before moving on. The drone of flies was everywhere and carcasses took on new life as the maggots jostled beneath the skin, picking them clean.

What was happening was merely a change in the cycle of nature, but man had imposed his will upon the wilderness. He had interfered with a natural environment and had not taken steps to counteract this. The carnage that ensued was a sight seldom seen in the wilderness before man's imposition.

Several years later, I found myself in a reserve where a decision to cull was reached and implemented. The cull was to be over a short period, but intense. In an open vehicle with a driver, spotter, marksman and a back-up marksman, I accompanied one of the first expeditions as an observer.

Starting out in the late afternoon, we had not travelled far when we came across a large herd of impala grazing a short distance from the road. The vehicle rolled quietly to a stop. Perhaps only half the group bothered to lift their heads and pay us any attention. The spotter surveyed the herd.

"Three," he said.

Three sharp cracks rang out, the last coming a little slower than the first two. The herd took to its heels and sprinted for a hundred and fifty metres, then stopped and turned back to stare in our direction.

Three impala lay dead. Perhaps the third victim knew there was danger, but the first two died without hearing the shot that killed them. It was death, but death without pain.

It so happened that that year became a drought year.

The sun beat down with all the ferocity I had experienced in the past, but grass still covered the ground. Animals lost condition and grew thin but this time I saw none of those pathetic skeletons teetering on emaciated legs.

Many months later the rain pattered softly on the dry grass, its gentle murmur whispering of relief. I had not seen one animal die the lingering death of starvation. The cull had also produced a large revenue which not only assisted the reserve in making a complete recovery but in further improvements as well.

Apart from the visible and tangible suffering of the animals, there is extreme pressure and severe damage to another sector of the reserve if culling is not implemented: the vegetation.

The destruction and retrogression that occurs to the vegetation of a reserve when it is denuded, is often paid insufficient heed.

How often I have heard, "But there is grass everywhere," when a year of good rains follows a bad drought. But grass is not just grass. There are hundreds of varieties that taste completely different from one another and have vastly different nutritional values.

Modern man is acutely aware of the make-up of the goods that he eats. The starches, proteins, minerals and vitamins that his body requires are widely publicized and often a major concern.

Yet man does not apply the same standards to the food wild animals consume. Accepting all vegetation as having the same nutritional value, is rather like comparing cooking fat and a prime fillet. They are both 'meat', but are vastly different.

In areas where the vegetation of a reserve has been stripped bare, it may take many, many years to attain its former state where it contained large numbers of species that were attractive to animals.

I reiterate that the fundamental component of any reserve is its vegetation and that the protection of that vegetation is a major priority.

There is an alternative to culling; the old man brought it home to me in another one of his stories, but I shall not relate it here for it is lengthy. Suffice it to say that he held this to be merely culling by another name. It is an activity that is both abhorred and loved; I talk of hunting.

I derive no pleasure from hunting. There is a thrill, that I cannot deny, but then I feel the same surge of adrenaline when stalking an animal with my camera.

Whatever his motivation, I do not feel that I can condemn another man who takes pleasure in an area where I do not. What a dull and mundane place the world would be if every man thought and acted alike. Man has always been, and still is, the ultimate predator. There is a latent natural instinct in all of us to hunt, but this is superseded by the pacifism instilled in us by society.

The hunter is in many instances a benefit to the wilderness. There comes a time in the life of any reserve when certain animals have to die to ensure the continued stable existence of the reserve. Now here is a man not only willing to do the job but prepared to pay handsomely for the privilege. An animal killed by a hunter generates a large amount of capital which can then be put back into the reserve.

As long as certain rules and principles are adhered to, and animal populations are not allowed to dwindle far below the level of normal stability – and I stress that these ethics must be maintained – I see no reason why animals should not be hunted. The hunter takes from a wilderness, but gives in return.

A question of economics: the conservationist would do well to consider that in a world whose population increases every minute, land is a dwindling resource. I do not wish to sound fatalistic, merely to acknowledge the fact that there are many who look with hungry eyes at land which lies dormant.

A National Park is perhaps the most secure wilderness when confronted by the pressures of an expanding world. It has been proclaimed a national heritage, to remain untouched. It can break free of the world of economics because the nation's coffers guarantee its support.

The same is not true of the reserves on the western boundary of the Kruger National Park. Owned by conglomerates of individuals and privately funded, these areas enjoy only some protection in their proclamation as Nature Reserves. However, this may prove scant security in the face of a determined drive for land. Sooner or later, and I feel that it will be sooner rather than later, these reserves will have to prove themselves capable of generating income and of maintaining their economic independence.

There is a multitude of options open to achieve this goal. Perhaps the most attractive is commercial tourism with the operation of game lodges and the conducting of safaris through the reserve. This form of utilization generates income far in excess of any other activity and it is a commercial venture that surpasses most farming in the capital invested and turnover. This alone provides strong justification for the continued existence of the wilderness that supports this industry.

With the accent on exclusivity and professionalism, people from all over the world are drawn to the reserves. Apart from the obvious monetary gains they bring, they also encourage widespread interest in the reserves, ensuring support for them both locally and internationally.

By the very nature of their work, these institutions also bring about an increase in conservation and wilderness awareness, heightening concern for such areas not only in southern Africa but worldwide.

Although an intrusion upon a wilderness, it is a relatively passive one. There are many who would prefer the wilderness without these intrusions but I am sure that they would agree that a wilderness with a passive intrusion is better than no wilderness at all.

Wilderness; wilderness and its preservation. To all those who are interested and involved I advocate caution. Caution, for we are dealing with something far greater than ourselves and we stand only on the threshold of understanding.

In conclusion, I quote Colonel J. Stevenson-Hamilton. 'Change and Evolution! They are nature's first laws; nothing may stagnate and still endure; but let us see to it that the changes are healthy, that the evolution proceeds on the right lines, that in our process of artificial development we do not so try to improve upon nature as to mar her fair works. Above all, let us not confuse progress with sordid commercial exploitation, as, alas! is too often the case.

'Let us, then, so far as in us lies, make it our duty to hand on this heritage of wild spaces and splendid animals intact to posterity.'

The evanescence of a bushveld rainbow
belies the fury of the storm it heralds.

A rising amber moon, snared for a moment in the thorny branches of a leafless acacia, bathes the wilderness and its whispering trees in its eerie light.

A malachite kingfisher pauses in the tireless quest for its silvery prey, bestowing a transient splash of colour to its swaying, dipping perch. Without warning, it will drop down to fly so close to the water that its passage ripples the surface, before rising again, abruptly, to alight on another favourite vantage point.

A hippopotamus yawns, stretching its massive jaws and revealing a fearsome array of weaponry. Impelled because of its sun-sensitive skin to seek the protection of its watery world, the hippopotamus will emerge at night to graze, consuming vast amounts before dawn drives it back to the water.

Right: With all the joie de vivre *of youth, two subadult cheetah cavort in a game that will teach them many of the skills later required for hunting.*

Below right: Another pair of youngsters stretch themselves to the full in determined pursuit of a herd of impala – a futile endeavour, since the antelope had seen them before they even began their stalk.

Far right: The frivolity of adolescence outgrown, an adult cheetah stands quietly on a fallen tree, using the added elevation to its advantage as it looks out over its sun-dappled domain.

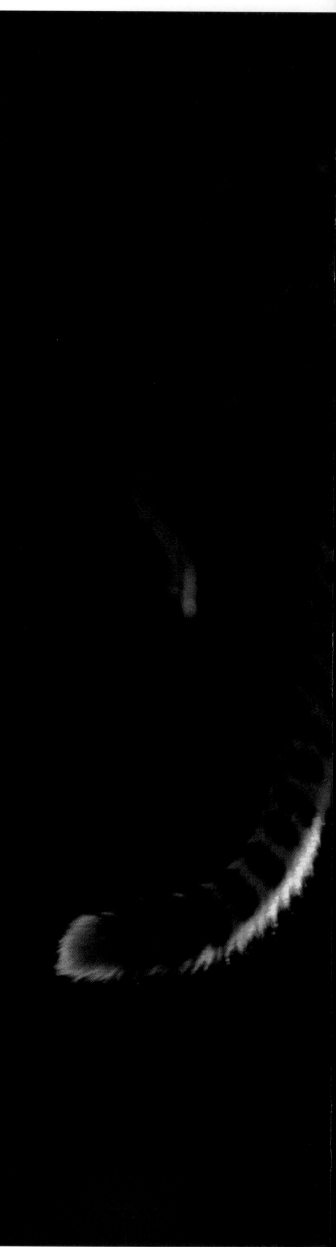

At times an animal is so at one with its environment that there exists between the two a momentary bond of exquisite delicacy, a bond so harmonious that the one would be wholly incomplete without the other.

38

Above: The last rays of a dying sun illuminate a late summer storm, setting fire to billowing mountains of water.

Below: Adherents to one of the classic laws of nature – that death perpetuates life – an impala stares through sightless eyes, its carcass destined to sustain its predator. The cheetah cub, though, appears somewhat bewildered, not knowing quite where to begin one of its first solid meals.

*Creating its own halo, the sun penetrates the chill of
an early morning mist that hangs, shroud-like, from
a long-dead leadwood tree.*

By all ye cry or whisper,
By all ye leave or do,
The silent, sullen peoples,
Shall weigh your Gods and you ...

Rudyard Kipling

The
BiSAND

'To promote and conserve wild life, fauna and flora ...' begin the objectives of the constitution of the Sabi Sand Game Reserve.

A group of five white rhino, grazing contentedly, their trumpet-like ears waving to and fro, bears mute testimony to the success of the reserve's objectives. Reintroduced some twenty years ago, they flourished in an area where they had not been seen since the middle of the last century.

Guided by enlightened management, a myriad forms of life, from the new green shoot to the elephant, endure in the 57 000 hectares of this sanctuary. Now silent and brooding, now bubbling with laughter as it dances between the rocks, the Sand River runs through the middle of the reserve. Moving away from its banks to the east, the reserve undulates in gently rolling hills until the boundary of the Kruger National Park is reached. To the south, the land climbs and then drops away, until the sonorous snort of the hippo announces that you have reached the Sabie River on the southern boundary. To the north and west, along plains and across koppies, a common boundary is shared with Gazankulu.

Oldest of the reserves, the first farm was purchased as a game farm in 1926. Over the years, the reserve grew and shrank, as farms joined and left, until a relative stability was reached.

In the early 1960s the Sabi Sand gained the official recognition that it sought and was proclaimed a Nature Reserve. Today several commercial tourist lodges flourish within the reserve, proving conclusively that a nature reserve can hold its own in the battle of commerce without damaging the intrinsic beauty of a natural realm.

The Sabi Sand is a tranquil reserve of gentle hills that are punctuated here and there by koppies of rock. Enjoying a comparatively high rainfall, a good summer produces a mantle of green, pervading the air with the peace and quiet of contentment. A cloak of yellow and gold embraces the reserve as owners come to enjoy the mild winters. A colonial flavour still lingers, to add intrigue to the majesty and serenity of a most special place.

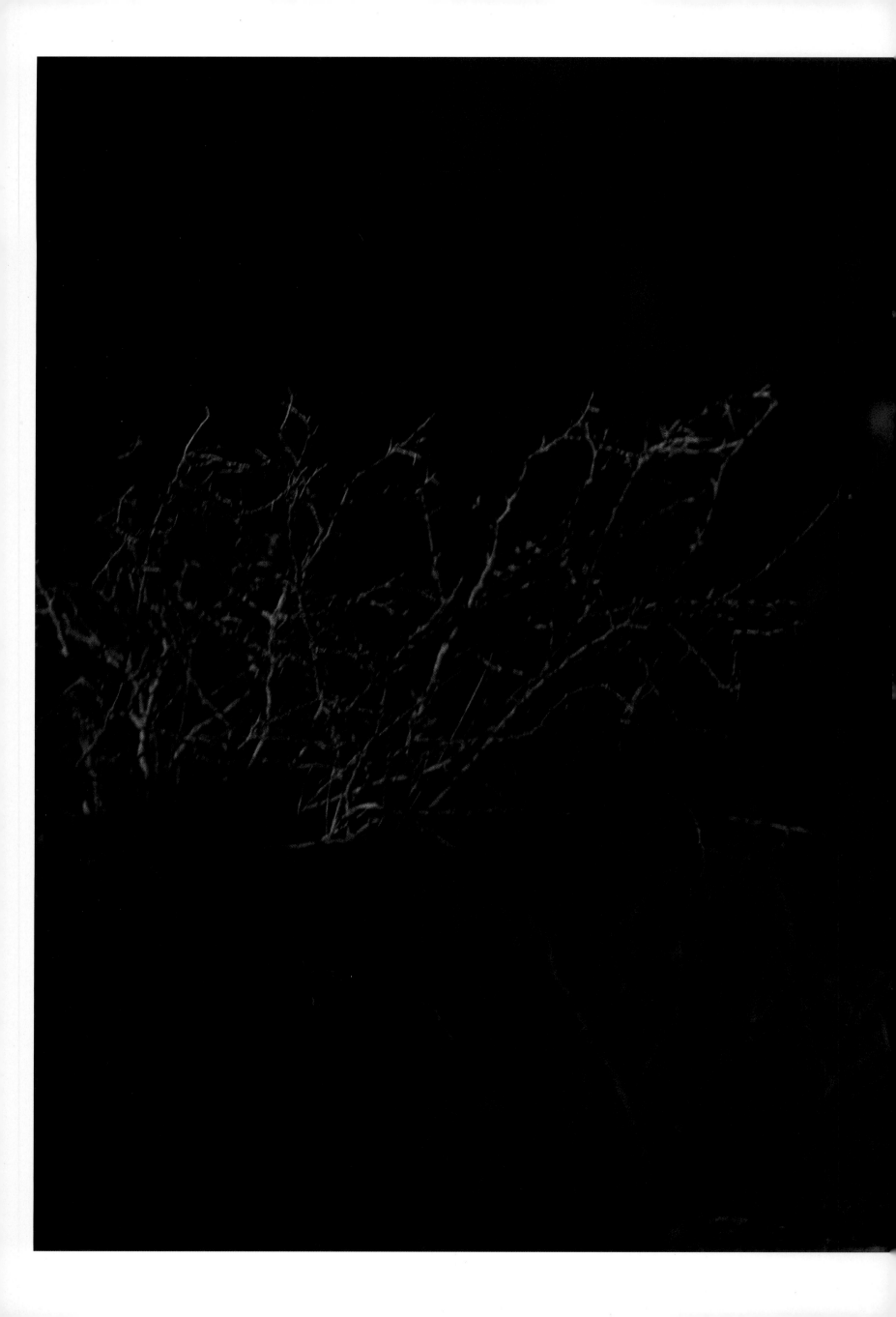

A young male impala stands rigid, every sense alert. Modern man has, by and large, forgotten what it is to live under the constant threat of death, where the merest misplaced sound causes heads to jerk up and sudden movements induce starts of apprehension. We have departed from the need to have our senses honed to the finest point and as a result have lost our empathy with the creatures of the wild.

On legs as slight and brittle as the branches of a fallen tree, two impala combine in a fleeting, graceful and seemingly effortless pas de deux.

A cheetah keeps a wary watch over the bush under which it has hidden its kill. It is not without its own fears: virtually all the other large predators are capable of chasing off this lightly built predator and expropriating its meal.

Forced to interrupt its meal at my approach, this tawny eagle fixed me with a stare of such blatant contempt and thinly veiled fury that I was obliged to retreat.

Like a droplet of rain caught within its own surface tension, a frog rests among the slender leaves of a reed. At night its liquid call, reminiscent of water dripping into a pond, delights the listener.

A master swordsman immaculate in his finery, this whitefronted bee-eater uses his rapier-like beak to snatch insects in mid-air with unerring accuracy.

With regal disregard for man's attempt to contain and confine, a kudu bull clears a two-metre fence with ease. It is a sobering thought that our achievements are recognized and lauded only by ourselves, and that, were we to pass from this earth, our creations would be passed by, unappreciated by the creatures of the world.

Raising their wings as their fervour increases, a pair of yellowbilled hornbills bounce up and down, rattling the branches of their perch as they perform a comical but endearing duet.

Silent, moving like a shadowy wraith, a full-maned lion pads along a palm-fronded dry river-course. Circular depressions in the soft sand provide the only evidence of his passing.

Framed by the rich green of summer, a bull buffalo sniffs indelicately at the breeze for signs of danger.

Piggy-back dinner guests: redbilled oxpeckers interrupt their search for ticks and other parasites as they sense their host's agitation. The grass that tickles the impalas' bellies could easily conceal a predator.

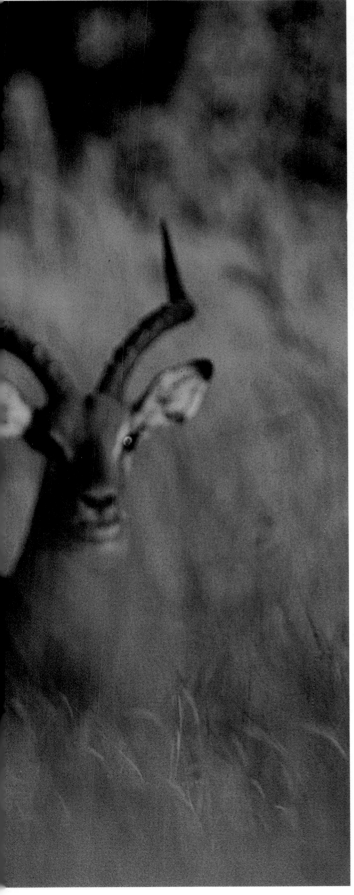

Finding comfort where none other could, this klipspringer appears completely relaxed on its bed of sharp, rocky ground.

A leopard cub creeps forward to peer through the foliage, feline curiosity overcoming its inherent shyness.

Previous page: A spider straddles the entrance to its home, which is festooned all too briefly with dew: the myriad droplets sparkle like gems in a light that, as it grows stronger, will soon enough destroy them.

In a dance beyond its control, the reflection of the moon wavers across the oily surface of the Sabie River.

Man's persecution brought the wild dog so close to the brink of extinction that even today it is still high on the list of endangered species.

The hunt and the kill: I heard, not saw, the paws rip at the earth as the lions accelerated. The lioness caught the wildebeest on the hindquarters and her impetus threw both into a frantic, tumbling heap. The wildebeest regained its footing but the lioness was quicker. She bit down and the wildebeest's screams were cut short, like a needle ripped from a record. Four minutes later the wildebeest lay dead, the lioness panting rasping gasps of air beside it.

This night will live with me forever: only once before had I witnessed such terror, and I still hear, and feel, the torment of that dying cry.

The wood owl's lilting call is one that tugs gently at the soul, evoking a sense of nostalgia for the magic of the bushveld night.

Sometimes one must stop in mid-stride, stand still and look carefully in order to notice the perfection that might otherwise be brushed aside or crushed by the next step.

There is no doubt that were Mother Nature left undisturbed
by man, she would soon strike a just balance among her
children, and no species, herbivorous or carnivorous,
would be permitted to increase to the detriment of others.
But let the balance be ever so little upset by artificial
means, and the whole delicate machine at once gets out
of gear and is difficult to re-adjust. It should be the aim
of a wildlife sanctuary to preserve nature's methods, for
only where these are strictly maintained is it possible
to acquire that true conception of the life
histories of the animals ...

Colonel J. Stevenson-Hamilton

The TIMBAVATI

There is a squeal of alarm, then an elephant's trumpeting rents the air as a matriarchal female comes to the protection of her young charge.

It was with less ado that the members of the Timbavati came to the rescue of their ailing wilderness. Realizing that only through preserving the basis of their reserve, the grass and the trees, could they preserve the living creatures, they decided to remove the excess animals that had created the imbalance.

Today the bush continues to improve in leaps and bounds. The money gained from a well implemented cropping scheme is ploughed back into the reserve – a classic example of the law of the wilderness, as death brings life.

A long narrow reserve, the Timbavati on its eastern border shares a common boundary of approximately forty kilometres with the Kruger National Park. To the west lie agricultural farms and other reserves, and to the south the Timbavati River which gives its name to the reserve. Flowing sporadically, its wide sandy bed supports still, silent pools that croak to life at night. Beds of tall reeds bend and rattle in the wind, keeping their secrets to themselves.

Further to the north, several dry river courses with palm-clad banks meander through the 62 000 hectares of the reserve. A number of tourist lodges dot the banks, catering to those who wish to feel the breath of the African wilderness. Here and there a dam wall spans the river beds and large expanses of water twinkle in the sunlight, calling a host of birds to their shores. The bleep of a radio tracking device might mingle with the bird calls, as members of the Hans Hoheisen Research Institute, situated in the south of the Timbavati, go about their work. With the full co-operation of the reserves they attempt to separate the wheat from the chaff as they study various animals.

At night the roar of one of the famous white lions floats on the air, announcing the Timbavati as his home, as many a man wishes he could.

Motionless, a great white egret confronts time with an attitude totally foreign to man. Gone is the urgency and pressure of counted seconds as time itself becomes timeless and life becomes its own measure.

A water leguaan gazes down from its rocky ledge with every appearance of contentment as the sun gathers strength, driving the night's chill from its bones.

Wily and cunning, the black-backed jackal is one of the few creatures to survive outside wilderness areas – despite all man's efforts to eradicate it. Although it scavenges when carrion is available, it is also a capable and efficient hunter.

Previous page: A herd of wildebeest erupts into panicked flight and redbilled oxpeckers take to the air, their chirruping lost in a confusion of splashing and snorting. Drinking is a time of extreme anxiety for animals as, with their heads down and backs to their escape route, they are at their most vulnerable.

Temporarily chained by droplets of dew, these feathery seeds will soon be borne off by the wind.

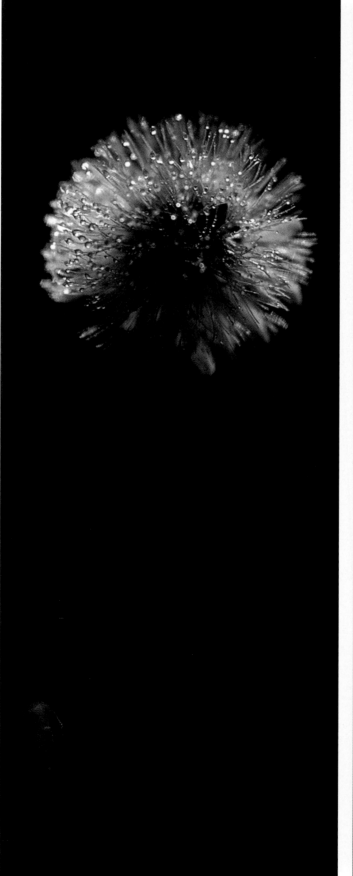

Left above: Dictator of the waterways, an Egyptian goose flies upriver, ready to hurl abuse at any creature that may violate its territorial rights.

In the waving beds of reeds that line the water, a host of other birds make their home. Their existence revealed, for the most part, only by the sounds they make, they may occasionally venture into the open to grace a fallen reed.

Death from excess. This acacia, killed by the rising waters of a dam, forms a resting place for a darter that will hunt for fish between rotting branches that once rustled gracefully in the wind.

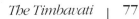

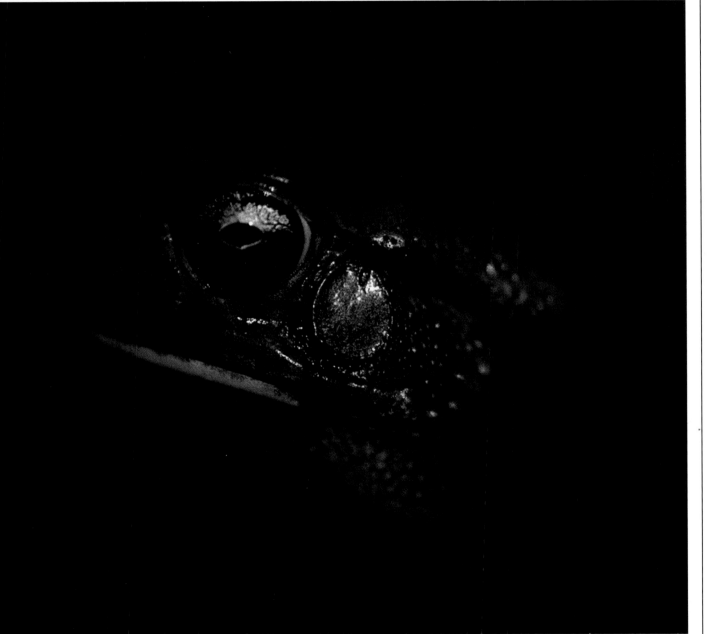

A ray of light reveals an olive toad in hiding as it awaits nightfall before setting forth in search of its insect prey.

Whitebacked vultures, stalwarts of caution and patience, lend ghoulish decoration to lifeless branches before descending to feed.

The stark form of a tree adds to the serenity of evening.

A white rhinoceros chews fitfully on grass stalks and a dry tamboti branch, while redbilled oxpeckers worry at its wounds, the result of a recent fight.

Hissing and cackling, slashing and flailing with claws capable of inflicting vicious wounds, two vultures rise into the air. In times when food is scarce, a carcass can become so competitive a prize for these birds that it vanishes completely beneath a seething mass of feathered bodies.

The antithesis of Narcissus, a threebanded plover appears wholly unaffected by the perfection of its image as it struts the bank in the stillness of early morning.

Man's encroachment has had a tragic impact on the blue wildebeest. Fences have cut across its migration routes and access to water, resulting in the agonizing, protracted death of thousands and forcing the adjustment of instinctive cycles that are centuries old.

Facing a more immediate danger is this hare, its eyes revealing the fear that courses through its body. Relying on its cryptic colouring and quiescence to avoid detection, it will burst into a racing zig-zag of speed only when it finds itself at the very extreme of risk.

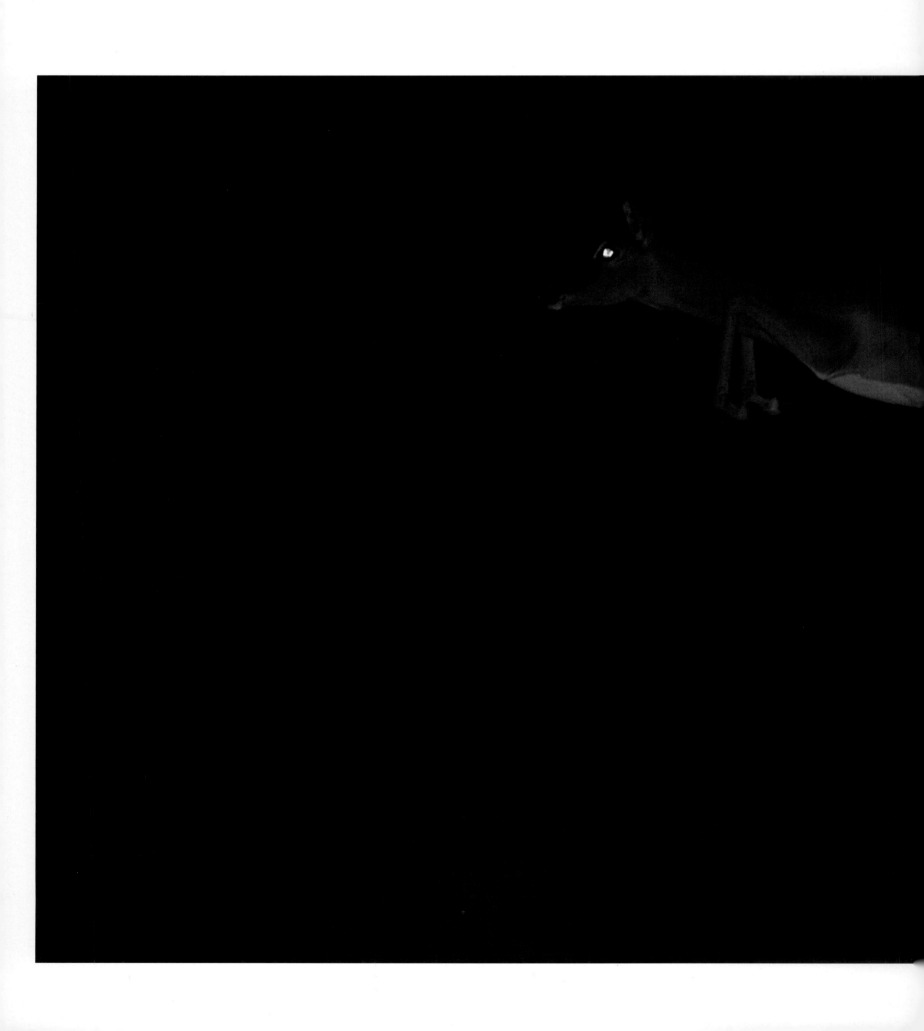

Spotlit on its own natural stage, a redeyed dove performs a subdued and rolling solo for the world.

The flash probes the veil of darkness to illuminate an impala as it lifts free of gravity.

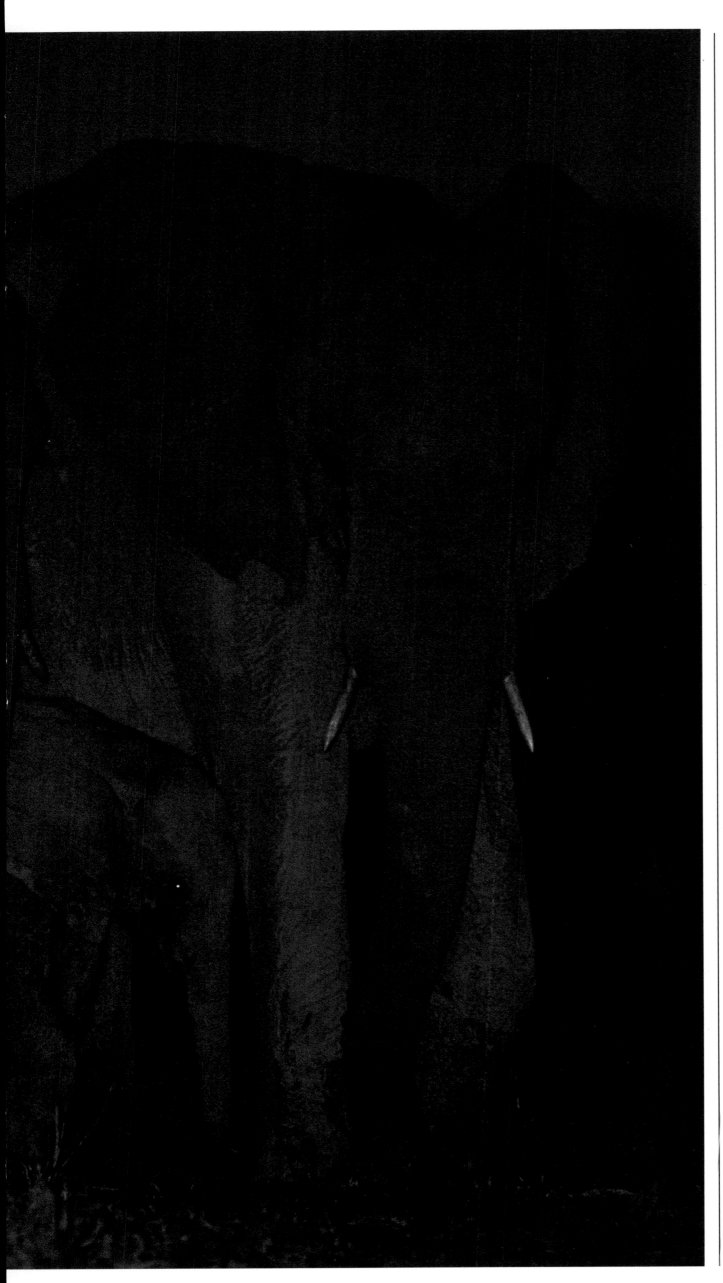

With feet that surely walked another world, these phantoms touched my conscious world and left in their wake the essence of Africa.

*Water's constant caress smoothes the roughness from
the surface of a rock.*

*Left: This young lion yawns expansively, adding its
guttural groan to the myriad sounds of the night.*

... but in her heart of hearts she is and remains wild and free and unaffected by the invading influences.

J.C. Smuts

The KLASERIE

Youngest of the reserves, the Klaserie was established in 1969. With some aggressive support and promotion by the owners, it was declared a Nature Reserve in the early 1970s.

It is an easy-going reserve where a friendly atmosphere prevails and old-fashioned courtesy and 'bush hospitality' may still be found.

The Klaserie River cuts a broad swathe as it meanders through the reserve, its wide, sandy bed clad in a waving blanket of tall green reeds. An elephant noisily drinks its fill from the meagre flow of water, unaware that progress might dry out this lifeblood of the reserve, as a dam on the Klaserie River is contemplated.

Offering a complete cross-section of vegetation, the reserve stretches south from the Olifants River, covering 60 000 hectares. The harsh, arid terrain of the northern part of the reserve is a mass of rocky outcrops and steep ravines. A raw, uncompromising wilderness where scorpions shuffle, and rock figs cling precariously to their stony perches.

Moving south, the reserve gradually becomes more hospitable until long, low, undulating hills mingle with wide, tree-speckled plains. Giraffes abound, their stately mottled forms blending with the muted colours of their surroundings. A programme of the capture and resale of these most extraordinary creatures helps generate revenue for a reserve that shies away from commercial tourism, allowing only one organization to conduct walking trails through its confines.

Several species have been reintroduced to the Klaserie. The stately sable and shy nyala tread cautiously down the paths of their return. On a cold, dew-laden morning the blurred image of a cheetah races the dawn in a land where wild is wild and free is free.

94

Emblem of wild Africa. The elephant's slide toward extinction has slowed and we congratulate ourselves on stilling our own greed.

The frangible, lace-like appearance of the dragon fly at rest is at odds with its ferocious predatory nature on the wing, when it engages in spectacular aerobatics while chasing its prey.

An inquisitive squirrel peeps out from the safety of its home.

Worrying the last of life from its exhausted victim, a subadult cheetah inexpertly applies the stranglehold that it must use to kill its larger prey.

Master of camouflage and of the silent stalk, a leopard hesitates, momentarily revealing itself in silhouette.

A small family group of elephants walks in single file: giants of the wilderness dwarfed by the wilderness itself.

The intense heat of midday oppresses the chatter of leaves, stills the buzzing wings of insects, and sends elephants in search of the cool relief of water.

Water of life and life of the water harmonize as a young dabchick catches droplets in its spiky, immature feathers.

Smallest of the southern African kingfishers, a pygmy kingfisher twists on its own axis as it makes a mid-flight adjustment to its dive.

Lions have the most compelling eyes: amber, intense, unwavering – and chilling.

Retracting its eyes to protect them, a foam nest frog literally leaps blindly between the branches of a tree. Its mottled brown colouring renders it almost invisible when set against the bark.

A hyaena, teeth bared, whirls on its attacker. The social hierarchy of the spotted hyaena, is unusual in that subadults are allowed virtually complete 'right of way' by adult males, a position they often abuse.

Herald of death, bringer of blessing upon the hunt: the superstitions surrounding the chameleon are many among the peoples of Africa. This individual would surely give some substance to belief as it sheds its skin to take on a startlingly bizarre appearance.

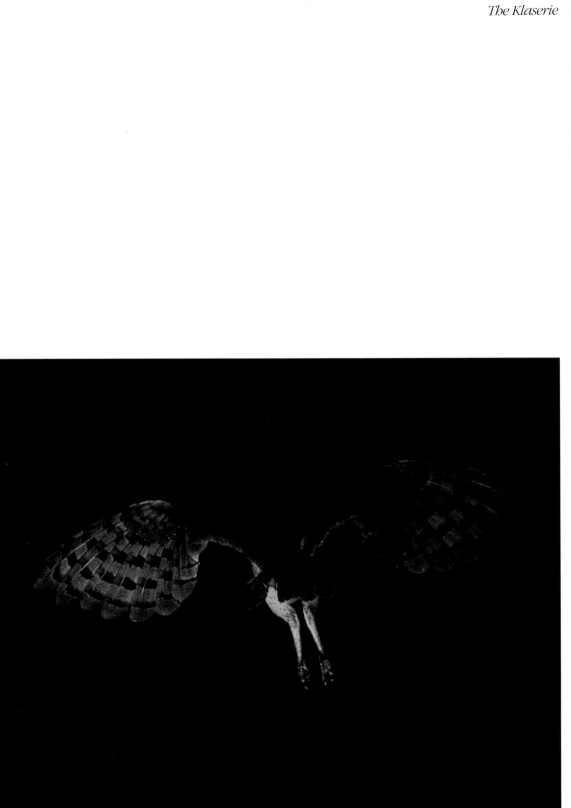

Making a mockery of darkness, a barn owl flies.

In a gesture universal among mammals, a cheetah cub seeks reassurance from its mother. When they first begin to follow their mother, cheetah cubs are extremely vulnerable and often fall victim to hyaena and other predators.

Overleaf: With inborn obedience, two cheetah cubs wait for their mother who has left them behind while she hunts. Using a bird-like, chirping call, she will eventually break their vigil and summon them to her.

Violence erupts as lions assert their rights over the remnants of a hippopotamus carcass. Unlike other gregarious animals, lions have a society based on a balance-of-power system, where violence between them is avoided because of the individual's ability to retaliate with violence. Virtually the only other mammal group with similar behavioural rules is the human race.

Swaying to the beat of their own hooves, giraffe gallop across a tree-studded plain.

Wearing the mottled uniform of the pack, three juvenile wild dogs trail a respectable distance behind their parents as they hunt. Among the most efficient of predators, wild dogs hunt co-operatively, chasing their prey until it is too exhausted to continue.

Top: Spring brings with it an intoxicating madness.

Diminutive farmer, an ant tends aphids and searches for other forms of food, in the process fertilizing the blooms on a stalk of grass.

Already swollen by pregnancy, this buffalo cow will wait for the winter to pass and the rich green of summer to blanket the wilderness before she is ready to give birth.

When a zebra filly comes into her first season she is a most flirtatious creature, blatantly tantalizing any male she happens across. In her presence, aggression between males runs high and often leads to serious fights, the participants inflicting vicious wounds on each other with their teeth and hooves.

Overleaf: 'Oh no! He's done it again,' these doublebanded sandgrouse seem to say as they give their call in melodious, subdued voices. Their legs hidden beneath their feathers, they give the impression of 'wind-up' toys as they creep between tussocks of grass.

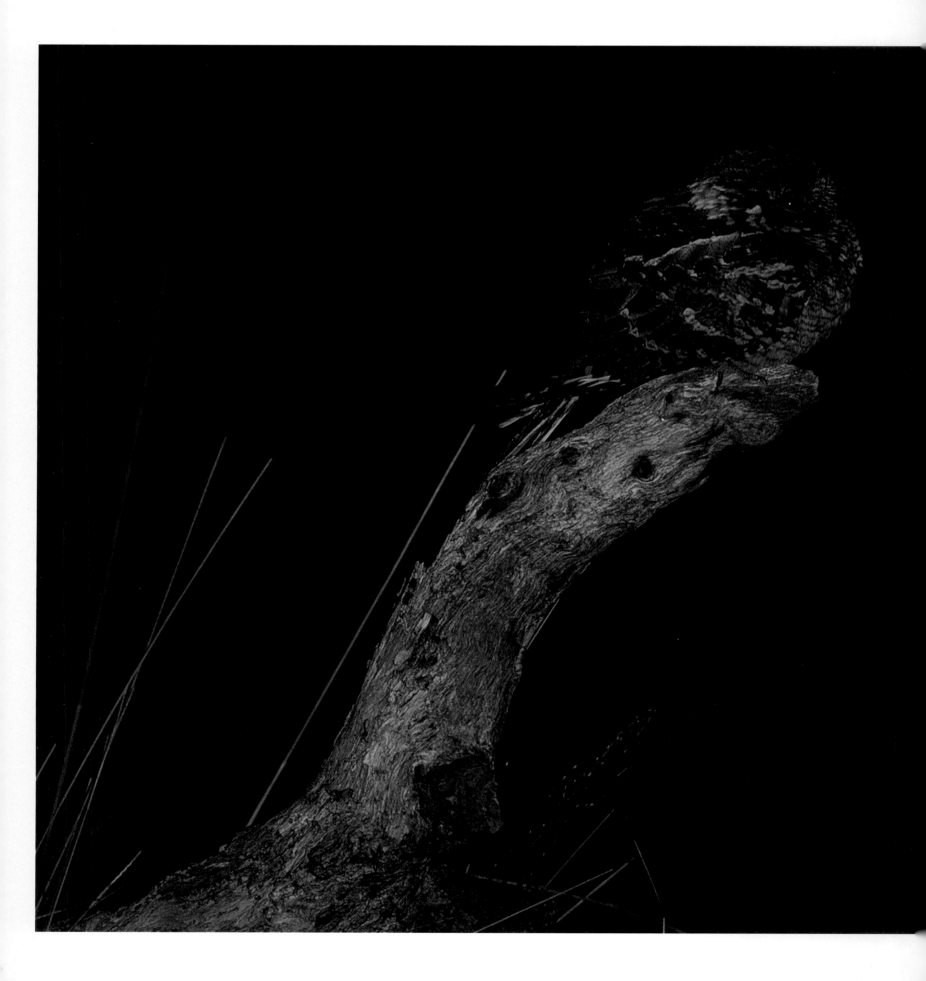

Frost glints as a grey duiker picks its way through the gossamer chill – a scene not normally associated with the African wild.

Left: One of the many pleasures of the wilderness is to sit in silence beside a campfire and listen to the call of the fierynecked nightjar.

Opening its hand-like feet, a lesser bushbaby prepares to land unerringly on a slender branch. With large, muscled hind legs that appear out of proportion to its tiny body, it is able to leap extraordinary distances between the tree tops that are its home. When forced to take to the ground it hops, comically, like a miniature kangaroo.

Devastation can be considered as either
an end or a beginning.

*Who can define the moods of wild places, the
meaning of nature beyond those of material use?
Here are worlds of experience beyond the world of
the aggressive man, beyond history and beyond
silence. The moods and qualities of nature and the
revelations of great art are equally difficult to
define; we can grasp them only in the depths of our
own perceptive spirit.*

Ansel Adams

*The spirit of the wild rests with African languor over the Kruger National Park.
For the most part it is gentle and benign, but it can also confront one with such
force that one is compelled to pause and reflect on the majesty of this vast
wilderness.*

*It was this majesty and spirit that touched President Kruger, after whom the park
is named, and prompted him to recognize the need for conservation. In 1898,
in the face of much opposition, he proclaimed the far eastern limits of his
republic a government reserve. During the first years of its existence, however, it
was observed more in contravention than obedience. Then, in 1902, a rather
diminutive figure arrived to take up his appointment as the first administrator
of this government reserve.*

*It is a strange comparison when one realizes that one million nine hundred
thousand hectares of protected wilderness could owe its existence to five foot
seven inches of man. It is however valid for, without the efforts of the
indefatigable Colonel James Stevenson-Hamilton, the Kruger National Park as
it is today would definitely not exist.*

*With the courage of his conviction, he faced seemingly insurmountable
opposition and with the tenacity of a honey badger fought for his beliefs. For
almost a quarter of a century Colonel Stevenson-Hamilton argued, defied,
cajoled and persuaded but never despaired. On the 31st of May, 1926 his
untiring efforts were rewarded when the then-Minister of Lands Mr Piet Grobler
proclaimed portions of the old Sabie and Shingwedzi reserves and the area
between them, the Kruger National Park.*

*The park encompasses an area 350 kilometres long and an average of 60
kilometres wide. A sizeable tract of land that could accommodate almost the
whole of Israel within its boundaries, it is today recognized as one of the top ten
National Parks in the world.*

*During the sixty years of its existence, the Kruger National Park has blossomed
and, through the unstinting efforts of many individuals, has earned an
enviable international reputation. Under the direction of the National Parks*

The KRUGER National Park

Board with its small army of staff, the Park follows a policy of minimum management for the wilderness under its jurisdiction. This allows the many different ecosystems within its bounds to follow their own natural course as far as possible, with man applying only the gentlest of guiding hands as he monitors its progress.

Across its length and breadth, a mosaic of ecosystems and vegetation types occur. To the north ancient baobabs predominate in a thirsty land of dusty red soil that receives less than 450 millimetres of rain a year. In stark contrast to these surroundings, Punda Maria rises above the plains, an island of lush denseness, and to the east the hills and rocky outcrops of the Lebombo Mountains give way to rolling plains.

Most of the transitions, however, are more gradual as mopane woodland with its fluttering green leaves gives way to the spiky-trunked knobthorn and the shade of the dappled marula tree. Forest degenerates to small trees and shrubs, eventually becoming rolling, tree-dotted plains. Dense riverine vegetation is hemmed in by thorny acacias, and as the hills around Malelaan rise more than 800 metres above sea level, they shake off all but the sturdiest of plant life.

As the plants vary, so do the animals and insects that thrive on them, resulting in a remarkable diversity of life. Many species that were endangered or locally extinct have been re-introduced and nurtured along the road to recovery. Others continue to struggle and their names hang precariously on the endangered species list. Today, however, over 130 species of mammal and more than 350 species of bird, including some spectacular migrants, can be found within the Park.

Although elsewhere science and 'progress' have caused much to vanish under their remorseless tread, in the Kruger this has been reversed as the complexities of nature have become increasingly understood and research provides direction. The second oldest National Park in Africa, the Kruger has faced tragedy, triumph and hardship on its forward path as it strives to protect a pristine wilderness and provide a glimpse of life detached from the greed of man.

Previous page: As the first stages of a drought left elephants with only a muddy pool, I marvelled at the quiet dignity of their suffering and wondered why I had never uttered a prayer for those that cannot speak.

Striped skinks, basking in the sun, add the symmetry of their own lines to that of a weathered log.

A dead acacia holds a little egret in its palm.

A tawny eagle launches itself into a diving swoop before rising to soar on thermals.

Even in the most peaceful settings of the wilderness, death is ever-present. Here impala drink from the crocodile-infested Pafuri River.

Africa has an ethereal quality: its breath whispers on plains of grass, its kiss tastes of dust, its progeny is special, and its spirit is bewitching.

Gliding effortlessly on their large wings, a pair of saddlebilled storks draw patterns of form and colour above the sandy banks of the Letaba River.

Legs outstretched, saddlebilled storks patter across the surface of the sand, folding their wings only when they have come to a complete halt.

Largest and arguably one of the ugliest of birds, the lappetfaced vulture with its bald head and thick beak is the dominant vulture species at a carcass.

Like a fingerprint, the zebra's stripes are unique to the individual. Males often have misaligned stripes – mute evidence of vicious injuries that have healed.

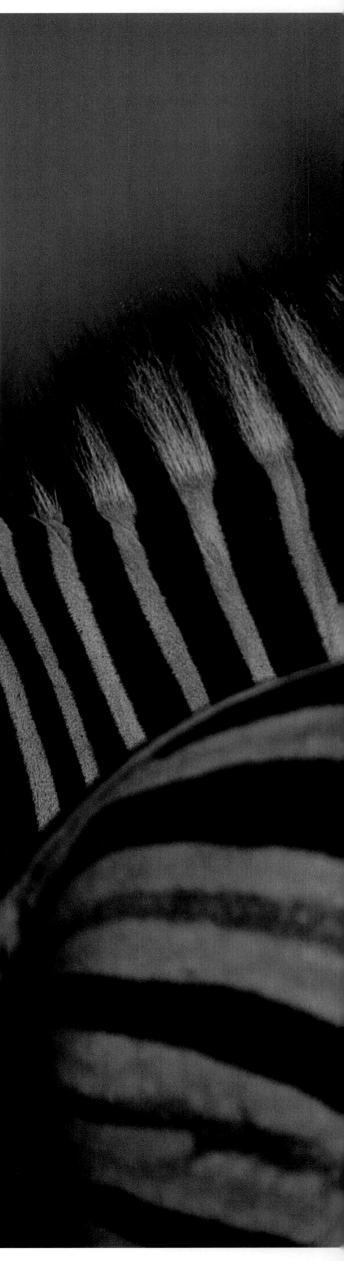

Having been driven from a pool which it tried to enter, a young hippopotamus lowers its head in submission at the approach of the dominant bull. Ignoring its subservience, the bull launches into the attack with his massive jaws agape. The sharp, tusk-like incisors slash at the youngster as it whirls around and tries to flee. Twice, before the young animal can make good its escape, the bull's teeth rake across it, cutting deeply, peeling shards of skin from the hide.

Paying scant heed to any territorial claims the hippopotamus may have, an elephant churns the water of the Olifants River. It moves between islets gathering trunkfuls of the spiky-leafed reeds that grow in profusion on the banks.

The camera, quicker than the eye, captures a pygmy kingfisher as it leaves a pool into which it has plunged for a quick bath.

Many of the world's great philosophers have turned to the wilderness to discover the fundamentals of life.

Although its reactions are fast enough to enable it to evade a striking snake, a dwarf mongoose nevertheless peers about cautiously before leaving the shelter of a termite mound.

The combined ears and eyes of a herd of impala, which bunches together for protection as night falls, make it extremely difficult for a predator to approach undetected.

A moon moth, clothed in finery, never feeds during its brief life as its mouthparts are sealed.

The eerie call of the black-backed jackal rises from the African plains.

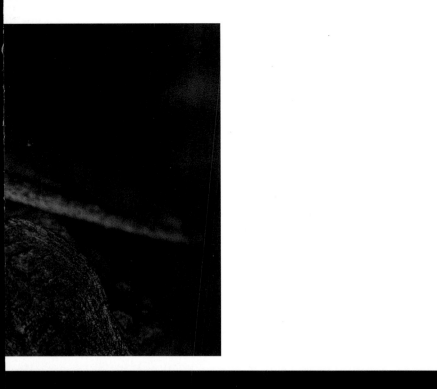

As the evening breeze tugs at the nodding heads of grass, a cheetah satisfies itself with its surroundings before settling down for the night.

The supremely agile leopard is completely at home in a tree. Using its claws and astounding strength, it is able to climb a vertical trunk carrying a kill in its mouth.

Hissing and spitting, a young leopard keeps its sibling at bay as it finishes a meal.

An impala ewe picks her way
delicately into a thicket
suffused with the orange
of evening.

To touch the wilderness once is always to carry a part
of it with you.

I passed through a paper village under glass
where the explorers first found
silence and taught it to speak

Richard Shelton